c.1
10⁰⁰

917.8
Seidman
    Once in the saddle: the
cowboy's frontier, 1866-1896

c.1
10,00

917.8   Seidman, Laurence Ivan, 1925-
S   Once in the saddle: the cowboy's
         frontier, 1866-1896. Illustrated with
         contemporary prints and photographs.
         New York, Knopf [1973]
             199 p. illus., maps, music. 22cm.
         (The Living history library)

         Includes bibliographical references.

             1. Cowboys. 2. Frontier and pioneer
cb   life. I.   Title. II. Series.
         F596.S35

CA
R
979.
032
SEI

For many centuries the Great Plains were the home of wandering Indian tribes who lived by hunting the buffalo.

At the end of the Civil War the white man moved swiftly westward into this ancient land. By 1872, the railroads, with their tracklaying and piledriving gangs, had driven their rails clear across Kansas. The buffalo were exterminated and the Indians swept onto reservations.

Drovers from Texas began to drive their cattle over long trails to the stockyards and cattle towns along these rail routes. Between 1860 and 1890 six million Longhorns passed over the trails. Thus the Cattle Kingdom came into being on the open grasslands. From the Plains, every year, tens of thousands of steers were hauled off to Chicago to feed the hungry industrial workers east of the Mississippi.

The Cattle Kingdom produced the last great epic of frontier life and the cowboy was its hero. Who was this cowboy, and where did he come from? What, in truth, was the nature of his experience as horseman, as human being, as worker in the meat industry?

In this book, Laurie Seidman, drawing from a rich reservoir of little-known memoirs and cowboys' autobiographies, tells us something fresh and significant about these people and the historical era that produced them.

The Living History Library

General Editor: John Anthony Scott

★

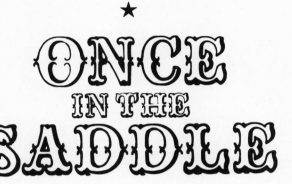

ONCE IN THE SADDLE

The Cowboy's Frontier 1866-1896

LAURENCE IVAN SEIDMAN

Illustrated with contemporary prints and photographs

ALFRED A. KNOPF : NEW YORK

For Mimi
whose encouragement and
help created this book.

Library of Congress Cataloging in Publication Data:

Seidman, Laurence Ivan, 1925– . Once in the saddle. (Living history library)

SUMMARY: Describes the life and work of the nineteenth-century cowboy, who became such a popular folk hero that his influence is still felt in American life. Bibliography: p. 1. Cowboys—Juvenile literature. 2. Frontier and pioneer life—The West—Juvenile literature. [1. Cowboys. 2. Frontier and pioneer life] I. Title. F596.S35 917.8 72-10425 ISBN 0-394-82013-4 ISBN 0-394-92013-9 (Gibraltar)

Manufactured in the United States of America

CONTENTS

ONCE
IN THE
SADDLE

INTRODUCTION

More than any other frontier figure, the cowboy has become our greatest folk hero, with a profound and continuing influence upon American life. Jeans, western shirts, boots, and Stetsons have become the national costume; the cowboy theme is endlessly repeated in our music, ballet, painting, and folklore. The cowboy's language has entered into our everyday speech in words like *stampede, cinch, roped in, rounded up, buffaloed, bawled out, tenderfoot.* Actors who have portrayed the cowboy, such as Roy Rogers, Gene Autry, and Hopalong Cassidy, have built personal fortunes and business enterprises worth millions of dollars. Almost one quarter of all the movies put out by Hollywood have been Westerns.

The most popular of all our folk figures, the cowboy has been romanticized, simplified, and stereotyped. Truth and fiction have been mixed together until he has become a myth, a timeless symbol of the West.

Why did the cowboy, rather than the logger, the forty-niner, the fur trapper, the buffalo hunter, or the cavalry soldier, capture the imagination of the American people?

Before the Civil War most Americans were farmers or craftsmen. They lived in the fields and the forests, in villages or in small towns. Business enterprise, where it existed, operated on a small scale. But by the 1880's this situation was changing with great speed. The North pulsated with new industrial power; factory production and railroad transportation were expanding at a tremendous rate. New cities were arising overnight to which swarmed millions of penniless immigrants. They toiled twelve to fourteen hours a day, six days a week, in the mines, mills, forges, tenements, and slaughterhouses. These workers, at their own risk, produced the wealth that made America rich and powerful. There was no job security; when men and women were laid off their families might starve. In Holyoke, Massachusetts, in the summer of 1873, the Holyoke *Transcript* reported:

There is one pitiful and miserable sight which we have seen night after night in front of the fruit and vegetable stands. . . . It is a drove of poverty-stricken children, often girls, clad only in one or two ragged and dirty garments, down on their hands and knees in the gutters, greedily picking out of the mud and dirt and eating the bits of spoiled and decaying fruit which have been thrown away as worthless.

These people lived jammed into tenements and slums. Lack of proper sanitation and the open sewers flowing through the towns generated epidemics of typhoid and diphtheria that swept away thousands of men, women, and children. Frequent fires in the rickety wooden buildings claimed many lives.

Thus industrial workers found themselves helpless

victims of their powerful bosses and of the unnatural environment in which they were obliged to live. The cowboy's existence, by contrast, was dignified, heroic, and free. Out on the vast prairie, men and women lived in a natural world and were masters of their own destiny. Perhaps this great difference between the sordid existence in the towns and the wild, free experience of the plains encouraged the workers to think of the cowboy's life as the true American ideal.

Even before the end of the great cattle drives and the life of the open range, the popular image of the cowboy was finding expression in print. John Baumann, who visited the West in the early 1880's and watched the cowboys at work, wrote an article in 1887 for an English magazine, *The Fortnightly Review,* in which he stressed the difference between the cowboy's actual existence and the idealized image of him that was becoming popular. "The cowboy," wrote Baumann,

has at the present time become a personage; nay, more, he is rapidly becoming a mythical one. Distance is doing for him what the lapse of time did for the heroes of antiquity. His admirers are investing him with all manner of romantic qualities.

Meanwhile the true character of the cowboy has been obscured, his genuine qualities are lost in fantastic tales of impossible daring and skill. . . . Every member of his class is pictured as a kind of Buffalo Bill, as a long-haired ruffian who, decked out in gaudy colors and tawdry ornaments, booted like a cavalier, chivalrous as a Paladin, his belt stuck full of knives and pistols, makes the world to resound with bluster and braggadoccio.

Thus, by 1890 the cowboy was becoming fair game for journalists in search of a story and for dime magazine writers who wanted to boost circulation. These people portrayed the cowboy as a fighter—quick to swear, swagger, and shoot. He was not an ordinary mortal, toiling long hours in mine or mill; he was a superman who didn't take it, but dished it out.

The clothes that the hero wore, the equipment he carried, and the horse he rode set him apart from ordinary folk. As historian Walter P. Webb put it in his classic work, *The Great Plains:*

"Ah," said the Easterner, "here is a new species of the genus homo. I must observe him carefully and note all his manners and peculiarities. There is something romantic about him. He lives on horseback as do the Bedouins; he fights on horseback, as did the knights of chivalry; he goes armed with a strange new weapon which he uses ambidextrously and precisely; he swears like a trooper, drinks like a fish, wears clothes like an actor, and fights like a devil. He is gracious to ladies, reserved toward strangers, generous to his friends and brutal to his enemies. He is a cowboy, a typical Westerner."

The first real Western novel appeared in 1902 and met with immediate and overwhelming success. It was Owen Wister's *The Virginian*. Every writer of Westerns from that day to this has followed Wister's scenario. The cowboy was portrayed as

a slim young giant more beautiful than pictures. His broad soft hat was pushed back; a loose-knotted, dull-

scarlet handkerchief sagged from his throat; and one casual thumb was hooked in the cartridge belt that slanted across his hips. He had plainly come many miles from somewhere across the vast horizon, as the dust upon him showed.

The hero is referred to throughout the book only as "the Virginian." He runs Judge Henry's Wyoming ranch, buys and sells cattle, rides the trails, and courts Molly Wood. Molly rescues him after an Indian fight and nurses him back to health with the aid of the local doctor ("Don't yu' let him die, Doc."). In the end Molly and "the Virginian" get married. He ends up as cattle magnate and mine owner, "an important man with a strong grip on many various enterprises, and able to give his wife all and more than she asked or desired."

The myth of the cowboy, of the wild open range, of the free life of rugged untamed men, has sustained Americans for many years, and indeed has achieved a timeless quality. By contrast, the actual western experience which gave rise to this myth was a very brief span of time indeed. The first herds traveled the western trails in 1866; the last herd went up the trail in 1896. Trail driving as an occupation and a business that produced the American cowboy lasted a mere thirty years before it vanished.

During these years cattle driving was organized upon a colossal scale. Frank Dobie, the great Texan historian and folklorist, believes that at a conservative estimate ten million Texas Longhorns and one million horses passed over the trails. The words of Walter Webb convey something of the magnitude of the drives:

As a livestock spectacle there has been nothing like it in America, unless it was the movement of the many millions of buffalo across the Plains; but with that man had nothing to do. . . . The cattle-ways from Texas were by no means the first. Cattle have followed wherever man has gone in this country. Cattle went to Oregon, to California, and over the Santa Fe trail long before the movement from Texas began. . . . But in all this, cattle were moving along with man for his convenience. They were but a detail, an incident to men's desire to get from one place to another. They moved because men moved. But in the drives from Texas man moved because the cattle had to move. The cattle were the main thing, not an incident. All else was incidental to them, even human life. With the cattle went no immigrants, no furniture or plows, no women or children, only men and horses and supplies for their immediate subsistence.

These Texas Longhorns, who were for thirty years the "main thing" in western life, are painted vividly in Frank Dobie's book, *The Longhorns:*

Tall, bony, coarse-headed, coarse-haired, flat-sided, thin-flanked, some of them grotesquely narrow-hipped, some with bodies so long that their backs swayed, big ears carved with outlandish designs, dewlaps hanging and swinging in rhythm with their energetic steps, their motley-colored sides as bold with brands as a relief map of the Grand Canyon—mightily antlered, wide-eyed, this herd of full-grown Texas steers might appear to a stranger seeing them for the first time as a parody of their kind. But however they appeared, with their steel hoofs, their long legs, their staglike muscles, their thick skins, their powerful horns, they could walk the roughest ground, cross the widest deserts, climb the highest mountains, swim the widest rivers, fight off the fiercest band of wolves, endure hunger, cold, thirst and punishment as few beasts of the earth have ever shown themselves capable of enduring.

In the myth the cowboy does not grow old. It is his glory to ride the range forever, brandishing his six-shooters, uttering his rebel yell, and carousing like Ulysses and his warriors in the towns along his way. What happened, though, to the real cowboys when the open range faded away and trail jobs became scarce? Cowboys went off in many different directions, but few of them became, like "the Virginian," successful magnates and mine-owners. Some filed on a homestead for 160 acres and became farmers or small ranchers. Others enlisted in the army, or went gold mining in Alaska, or found work in San Francisco's shipyards, in Montana's banks, in Denver's shops, in the lumber mills of Puget Sound. Many went back East to Chicago's factories and stockyards or New England's mills or anywhere that a suitable job might be found. Still others stayed in the small western towns to run hotels, to sell dry goods, or to work in the livery barns. A few ran for sheriff or Congressman, were appointed postmasters, became lawyers and tax assessors.

How did these men view their cowboy past? Many of them looked back on the experience with longing and regret. The life of the trails had not brought them wealth or affluence but it had been a full and vivid experience. G. D. Burrows of Del Rio, Texas, an old trail hand, writes in *Trail Drivers of Texas:*

Cowboy portrait. Seated are Wild Bill Hickok
(l.) and Buffalo Bill Cody. Standing is Texas
Jack Omohundro.

I had my share of the ups and downs, principally downs, on the old cattle trails. Some of my experiences were going hungry, getting wet and cold, riding sore-backed horses, going to sleep on hard ground, losing cattle, getting "cussed" by the boss. . . . But all of these were forgotten when we delivered our herd and started back to grand old Texas. . . . I always had the "big time" when I arrived in good old Santone, rigged out with a pair of high-heeled boots and striped breeches, and about $6.30 worth of other clothes. . . . This "big time" would last but for a few days, however, for I would soon be "busted" and would have to borrow money to get out to the ranch, where I would put in the fall and winter telling about the big things I had seen up North. The next spring I would have the same old trip, the same old things would happen in the same old way, and with the same old wind-up. I put in eighteen or twenty years on the trail, and all I had in the final outcome was the high-heeled boots, the striped pants and about $4.80 of other clothing, so there you are.

The cowpuncher, then, was a working man who lived a hard and often dangerous life, but who had his share of joy, and above all the joy of brotherhood. Ex-cowboy Teddy Blue sums it up:

A man has got to be at least 75 years old to be a real old cowhand. I started young and am 78. Only a few of us are left now and they are scattered from Texas to Canada. The rest have left the wagon and gone ahead across the big divide, looking for a new range. I hope they find good water and plenty of grass. But wherever they are is where I want to go.

The actual, historic experience of the men and women who lived on the western ranges and operated the cattle business in the years 1866–1896—this is the theme of the chapters that follow.

I Ride an Old Paint

Guitar introduction I

ride an old paint,— I lead an old dam,— I'm

goin' to Mon-tan - a to throw the hoo-li-han. They

feed in the coul-ees, they wat-er in the draw, Their

tails are all mat-ted, their backs are all raw.

Chorus

Ride a-round, lit-tle dog-ies, ride a-

round___ them__ slow, for the fie-ry and snuf-fy are

rar - in' to go. Ride a - rar - in' to go

I ride an old paint, I lead an old dam,
I'm goin' to Montana to throw the hoolihan.
They feed in the coulees, they water in the draw,
Their tails are all matted, their backs are all raw.

REFRAIN:
Ride around, little dogies,
Ride around them slow,
For the fiery and snuffy
Are rarin' to go.

Old Bill Jones had two daughters and a song,
One went to Denver and the other went wrong.
His wife she died in a poolroom fight,
Still he sings from morning till night.

REFRAIN

Oh, when I die, take my saddle from the wall,
Put it on my pony, and lead him from his stall.
Tie my bones to his back, turn our faces to the West,
And we'll ride the prairie that we love the best.

REFRAIN

THE GREAT PLAINS

The huge section of the United States that stretches from the Mississippi Valley to the foothills of the Rockies, from the Rio Grande to the Canadian border, is known as the Great Plains. It is an area of almost boundless extent covering nearly one fifth of the U.S.A. The Great Plains are largely treeless except along the water courses of the rivers, for the annual rainfall in this land is quite low—enough to sustain a cover of grass, but not the majestic trees that flourish in the eastern part of our country. These prairies, rolling in gentle sweeps as far as the eye can follow, resemble nothing so much as the ocean. Within their boundaries are to be found portions of ten states: Colorado, Montana, New Mexico, Wyoming, the Dakotas, Kansas, Nebraska, Oklahoma and Texas.

Seventy-five years before the English landed at Jamestown, the Spanish were exploring the southern part of this region. Starting from Mexico, an expedition led by Francisco Vasquez de Coronado roamed through New Mexico, Arizona, Texas, Kansas, and Oklahoma. The Spaniards were looking for the legendary golden cities

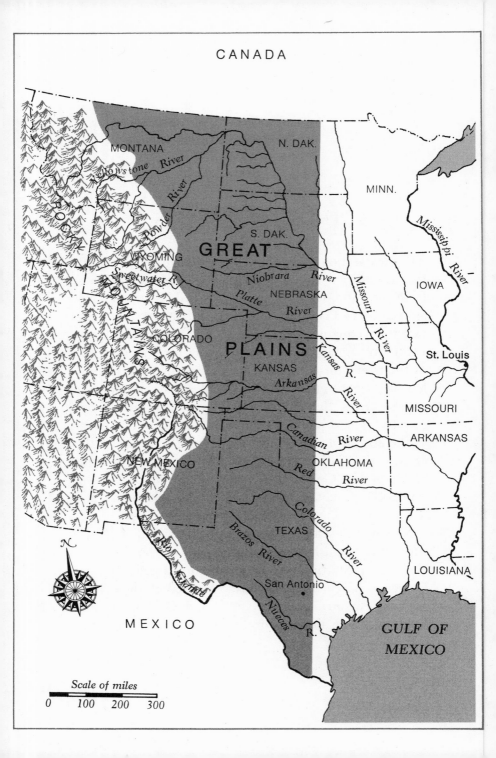

of Cibola and the riches with which they were supposed to be crammed.

One of Coronado's soldiers, Pedro de Castanada, recorded his memories of the two years of wandering:

The country is spacious and level. No settlements were seen anywhere on these plains. In traversing 250 leagues the other mountain range was not seen, nor a hill nor hillock which was three times as high as a man. Several lakes were found at intervals; they were round as plates, a stone's throw or more across, some fresh and some salt. The grass grows tall near these lakes; away from them it is very short, a span or less. The country is like a bowl, so that when a man sits down the horizon surrounds him all around at the distance of a musket shot.

Grass was the dominant form of vegetation. Men and animals passing through it made no more impression upon it than a ship that plows the ocean.

Who could believe that 1,000 horses and 500 of our cows and more than 5,000 rams and ewes and more than 1,500 friendly Indians and servants, in traveling over those plains, would leave no more trace where they had passed than if nothing had been there—so that it was necessary to make piles of bones and cow dung now and then, so that the rear guard could follow the army. The grass never failed to become erect after it had been trodden down, and, although it was short, it was as green and straight as before.

Coronado himself noticed the possibilities of this land for cattle-raising, commenting in a letter that "there is very fine pasture land, with good grass."

The Spaniards penetrated northward as far as Kansas and then returned to Mexico. They did not find the legendary cities of Cibola, but they encountered the buffalo and met some of the Indian peoples who inhabited the Plains.

Castanada described the buffalo, saying that they were "the most monstrous thing in the way of animals which has even been seen or read about." He noted that

There was not one of the horses that did not take flight when he saw them first, for they have a narrow, short face, the brow two palms across from eye to eye, the eyes sticking out at the side, so that when they are running, they can see what is following them. They have very long beards, like goats, and when they are running they throw their heads back with the beard dragging on the ground. They have a real hump, larger than a camel's.

Many different tribes of native American peoples lived scattered throughout the Plains. These peoples varied much in appearance, language, and religion, but they had many cultural traits in common since they were living in and adapting to a similar environment. Almost all of them were dependent upon the buffalo; to the native Americans this animal was life itself. One of the Spaniards with Coronado illustrated this fact vividly in a letter written in 1541:

With the buffalo skins they make their houses, with the skins they clothe and shoe themselves; of the skins they make thread with which they sew their clothes and also their houses [tents]. From the bones they make awls; the dung serves them for wood, because there is

"The Buffalo Hunt," a painting by George
Catlin.

*nothing else in that country. The stomachs serve them
for pitchers, vessels from which they drink. They live on
the flesh; they sometimes eat it roasted and warmed over
the dung, at other times raw.*

When the Spaniards arrived, then, the peoples of the
Plains were hunters and nomads; they did not cultivate
the soil, or grow corn or vegetables. The horse was entirely unknown to them. When the Spaniards appeared
on horseback the Indians fled in terror from these strange
new creatures. They had domesticated the dog; he was
their only beast of burden.

*People follow the buffaloes, hunting them. They travel
like the Arabs with their tents and troops of dogs loaded
with poles [i.e. travois] and having Moorish pack saddles
with girths. When the loads get disarranged the dogs
howl, calling someone to fix them right.*

By the beginning of the seventeenth century, the
Spaniards were establishing settlements in New Mexico
and Arizona. Their priests built missions and taught the
Indians how to farm and how to raise cattle and sheep.
But the main thing that the native peoples of the Plains
—Comanches, Cheyennes, Apaches, Pawnees, Sioux, and
other tribes—took from the Spanish was the horse. Raid-
ing the settlements in the south, they returned to the
Plains with herds of horses. Many Spanish steeds also
escaped from their masters and ran off to the Plains
where they found a natural pasture largely free of preda-
tory enemies. There they multiplied and became wild;
great herds fanned out over the prairies.

As for the peoples of the Plains, their whole way of

"Wild Horses at Play," a lithograph by George
Catlin.

life was transformed by the horse. Soon the nomads, who had wandered after the buffalo and hunted him on foot, became mounted warriors who ruled the Great Plains and rode as though born to the saddle. William Blackmore, an Englishman who spent eight years in the region, has left this description of the Comanches:

On foot slow and awkward, but on horseback graceful, they are the most expert and daring riders in the world. In battle they sweep down upon their enemies with terrific yells, and concealing the whole body with the exception of one foot behind their horses, discharge bullets or arrows over and under the animal's neck rapidly and accurately. Each has his favorite warhorse, which he regards with great affection, and only mounts when he goes to battle. Even the women are daring riders and hunters, lassoing antelope and shooting buffalo.

For almost 300 years Spain claimed possession of the Great Plains. It was an empty claim because the real rulers of the Plains were the independent and unconquered native peoples. In 1800 Spain turned over its claims to the French, who, by the Louisiana Purchase of 1803, sold them in turn to President Jefferson and the United States.

In 1804 Jefferson sent out Meriwether Lewis and William Clark to make their famous exploration of the Plains region. Their report attracted the attention of many others. In the years following, bands of fur traders and trappers, botanists, missionaries, observers, and private adventurers poured into the area in an ever-increasing flow.

The prairies abounded with game. The lands west of the Mississippi were a hunter's and trapper's paradise. James Pattie, a trapper who wandered through the Plains between 1824 and 1830, told of their richness in wildlife.

Finding a lake we encamped for the night. From this spot we saw one of the most beautiful landscapes that ever spread out to the eye. As far as the plain was visible in all directions, innumerable herds of wild horses, buffaloes, antelopes, deer, elk and wolves fed in their wild and fierce freedom.

The skies above the prairies were filled with huge flocks of game birds and a great variety of smaller songsters. Colonel Dodge, a western trapper and explorer, has left us this picture:

About the middle of September, the great Arctic breeding places began to pour upon the Plains migrating millions of water fowl of every variety, from the uncouth pelican to the smallest of sandpipers, geese of several kinds, ducks in wonderful variety, plover in half a dozen varieties, snipe, etc. Some of these stop for longer or shorter periods on every stream, and it is not until the icy hand of winter has closed the water courses that all disappear.

Three hundred years after Coronado, the American explorers of the High Plains found that the life of the Indian peoples still centered around the buffalo. These explorers brought back vivid pictures of the Plains folk whom they encountered in their journeys. Their way of life was quite different from that of whites, and was shaped by the environment in which they lived. The Plains Indians, for the most part, were nomadic, or wandering, hunters and food-gatherers.

Mobility, or nomadism, was the core of Plains Indian culture and enabled the people to survive the harsh conditions of the Plains environment. Their weapons were the bow and arrow and the stone-tipped spear or lance— weapons especially suitable for hunting the bison, elk, and other game.

Hospitality and courtesy to the stranger who came in peace was a strict rule among almost all the Indian tribes. John Bradbury, who traveled through the High Plains in the years 1810–1812, testified to this in his journal:

No people on earth discharge the duties of hospitality with more goodwill than the Indians. On entering a lodge I was always met by the master, who first shook hands with me, and immediately looked for his pipe; before he had time to light it, a bearskin, or that of a buffalo, was spread for me to sit on, although they sat on the bare ground. When the pipe was lighted, he smoked a few whiffs, and then handed it to me after which it went round to all the men in the lodge. Whilst this was going on the squaw prepared something to eat, which, when ready, was placed before me on the ground. The squaw, in some instances, examined my dress, and in particular my moccasins. If any repair was wanting, she brought a small leather bag, in which she kept her awls and split sinews, and put it to rights. After conversing as well as we could by signs, if it was near night, I was made to understand that a bed was at my service;

A Sioux warrior as painted by Carl Bodmer.

and in general this offer was accompanied by that of a bedfellow.

Indian people delighted in sports of all kinds. They played lacrosse and other ball games, and enjoyed gambling with dice. They loved horse races, on which everyone laid bets. The children, like children everywhere, had hoops, bows and arrows, and dolls. Men occupied themselves with hunting, tribal government, and making war. The rest of the necessary work fell to the women: preserving the buffalo meat, cleaning the skins, making clothes, putting up and taking down the tipis.

Francis Parkman, famous explorer and historian, described a group of Indians crossing a river to visit Fort Laramie. He noted their merriment and their joy in life:

Men and boys, naked and dashing eagerly through the water, horses with lodge poles dragging through squaws and children and sometimes a litter of puppies; gaily attired squaws, leading the horses of their lords; dogs with their burdens attached swimming among the horses and mules; dogs barking, horses breaking loose, children laughing and shouting . . . naked and splendidly formed men passing and repassing through the swift water.

The Plains Indians were warlike people; war, indeed was an important and a permanent feature of their way of life. Most of the tribes had hereditary enemies, that is to say, other tribes with whom they waged a never-ending struggle. Victories were celebrated with music, dancing, and feasting; losses with wailing and weeping.

Brackenridge, who explored the West in 1811, paints

a colorful picture of the return of an Arikara war party that had been victorious in a battle with the Sioux:

> They advanced in regular procession, with a slow step and solemn music. . . . The warriors were dressed in a variety of ways, with their cinture and crown of feathers, bearing their war clubs, guns, bows and arrows, and painted shields; each platoon having its musicians, while the whole joined in the song and step together, with great precision. In each band there were scalps fastened to long poles.

People flowed out of the village to welcome the returning warriors and to care for the wounded:

> Fathers, mothers, wives, brothers, sisters caressed each other without interrupting for a moment the regularity and order of the procession, or the solemnity of the song and step. I was particularly touched with the tenderness of a woman who met her son, a youth reported badly wounded, but who exerted himself to keep on his horse. She threw her arms round him and wept aloud. . . . As they drew near the village, the old people, who could barely walk, withered by extreme age, came out like feeble grasshoppers, singing their shrill songs, and rubbing the warriors with their hands. The day was spent in festivity by the village in general, and in grief by those who had lost their relatives.

White travelers admired the skill with which the Indian peoples had learned to adapt to the harsh Plains environment and to survive in it. They stressed the hardships and obstacles in the way of white settlement.

Buffalo Dance of the Mandan Indians, a tribe
from the Dakotas.

Francis Parkman described the land he saw in 1846 while traveling up the valley of the Platte River:

Before and behind us the level monotony of the plain was unbroken as far as the eye could reach. Sometimes it glared in the sun, an expanse of hot, bare sand; sometimes it was veiled by long coarse grass. Skulls and whitening bones of buffalo were scattered everywhere. The river itself runs through the midst, a thin sheet of rapid, turbid water, half a mile wide and scarcely two feet deep. Its low banks, for the most part without a bush or tree, are of loose sand, with which the stream is so charged that it grates the teeth in drinking.

One of the biggest obstacles to settlement was the lack of water. When rain did come, it fell in drenching sheets. Most of the water was not retained by the soil, but quickly ran off or evaporated into the hot and arid air. Rivers that were raging torrents one day dwindled away into shallow streams the next; they dried up entirely during the summer.

Another unpleasant feature of the Plains was the high diurnal range; that is to say, it might be very hot by day but freezing by night. In the summer, again, temperatures might rise to 100° or more; during the winter the thermometer might plunge to 20° or 30° below zero. Terrible blizzards, lasting for days, might take the lives of any travelers unfortunate enough to be caught out in the open.

Winds on the Great Plains blew more fiercely and constantly than in any other part of the United States. People's lips would burn, smart, and crack in the heat of the summer gale and their throats would become parched.

Thus the Great Plains presented such a contrast to the forested lands east of the Mississippi that the white settler found them uninviting. The pioneer's axe, boat, and wooden plow—tools with which he had mastered the eastern forests and the prairies of Illinois and Iowa—were not adequate to the conquest of this new and strange environment.

After 1830 Americans crossed the Great Plains in ever-increasing numbers, but they did not settle. Along the Oregon and California trails they plodded, anxious to reach the well-timbered and well-watered regions of the Pacific Coast, or to get to the gold fields. The Great Plains were simply a barrier that lay between them and the fulfilment of their dreams; they meant blizzards, howling storms, hunger and thirst, hostile Indians. There arose in the American mind the myth of the "Great American Desert" as

a boundless, trackless, worthless area, fit only for savage Indians and wild beasts, a land of cactus and prairie dogs, of shifting sands and tall eccentric whirlwinds of dust.

And so, too, it was marked upon the maps of that day. Colonel Dodge wrote:

When I was a schoolboy my map of the United States showed between the Mississippi River and the Rocky Mountains a long and broad white blotch upon which was printed in small capitals, THE GREAT AMERICAN DESERT—UNEXPLORED.

This "Great American Desert" was the United States'

last frontier. After the Civil War this section would be both explored and exploited. Whites would find that it had many profitable uses—once the Indian and the buffalo had been removed.

The Sprig of Thyme

wise, be - ware, keep your gar - den clear, Let

no man steal your __ thyme, _____ Let __

Verses 1-6

no man steal your __ thyme. For

Last verse

Come all ye maids where-e'er you be,
Who flourish in your prime,
Be wise, be-ware, keep your garden clear,
Let no man steal your thyme,
Let no man steal your thyme.

For when your thyme is pulled and gone,
They care no more for you,
There is not a place your thyme goes waste
But it spreads all o'er with rue,
It spreads all o'er with rue.

When I was a maid both fair and coy
I flourished in my prime,
Till a proper young man came and
He stole this heart of mine,
He stole this heart of mine.

My parents they were angry
At my being led astray,
But there's many a dark and cloudy morn
Brings forth a pleasant day,
Brings forth a pleasant day.

The gardener's son being standing by
Three gifts he gave to me,
The bitter rue, the violet blue
And the red rose it was three,
The red rose it was three.

Now I'll cut off the red rose top
And I'll plant on the willow tree,
That the whole world may plainly see
How my love slighted me,
How my love slighted me.

The begotten virgins they must live
Although they live in pain:
But the grass that is mown on yonder hill
Through time will bloom again,
Through thyme will bloom again.

THE CRADLE OF THE
CATTLE KINGDOM

Wherever the Spaniards went in the New World they took cattle with them. Richard Tomson, an Englishman who had been traveling with the Spanish for many years, told in a letter home in 1555 of the livestock of New Spain:

There is in New Spain a marvelous increase of cattell which dayly do increase and they are of greater growth than ours. You may have a great steer that hath a hundred weight of tallow for sixteen shillings and some one man hath 20,000 head of cattell of his own.

By 1650, when the English colonies in America were still largely wilderness, cattle raising was prospering in Mexico. Ships filled with hides as well as silver crossed the broad Atlantic to enrich the merchants and the Crown of Spain.

In 1821 a colony of Anglo-Americans led by Stephen F. Austin immigrated to Mexico with the permission of the Mexican government. They settled along the fertile and well-timbered valleys of the Brazos and Colorado rivers, and devoted themselves almost exclusively to raising stock.

Austin and his band had settled in the southeastern portion of the Mexican province of Texas; this, since Spanish times, had been the cradle of the American cattle industry. W. P. Webb describes the region as a diamond-shaped area with San Antonio at its northern apex and the Gulf of Mexico and the Rio Grande forming its southern boundaries.

This diamond-shaped region offered almost perfect conditions for the raising of cattle. The country was open, with mottes of timber offering shade and protection. Grass was plentiful, and in parts remained green throughout the year. The climate was mild, almost tropical, and there was neither snow nor blizzard, though an occasional norther swept down, only to fade and fail under the benign influences of the southern sun and the warm Gulf. The region was fairly well watered, particularly in the beautiful Nueces Valley, through which ran a living stream bordered by natural parks; but, what was more important, because of its position it was sheltered from the inroads of the Plains Indians.

Thus the San Antonio Valley became the prime breeding ground of the Texas Longhorns, a breed derived from crossing British cattle with Spanish cattle, which were mainly of Andalusian stock. By 1835 three million head of sheep, goats, horses, and cattle were counted in Texas, including huge numbers of cattle that roamed wild.

The last frontier of the American West, the cowboy's

frontier, was deeply affected by Spanish lifestyles and customs. Texas remained under Spanish rule until 1836. During this period the Texan "Anglos" learned much about ranching, and almost all that they learned came from the Mexican *vaqueros*. Vaquero means "one who works with cows," and it was Americanized as *buckaroo*. The vaqueros taught the Anglos riding, roping, trailing, and branding. The vaqueros invented and perfected the use of the lariat, an indispensable tool of the rancher's trade. Captain Basil Hall, an English traveler, described the vaqueros in 1824 as he watched them round up cattle and perform feats of lassoing:

The unerring precision with which the lasso is thrown is perfectly astonishing, and to one who sees it for the first time, has a very magical appearance. Even when standing still it is by no means an easy thing to throw the lasso; but the difficulty is vastly increased when it comes to be used on horseback and at a gallop, and when, in addition, the rider has to pass over uneven ground, and to leap hedges and ditches in his course; yet such is their dexterity that they are not only sure of catching the animal but they can place their lasso on any particular part they please; over the horns, round the neck or the body, or they can include all four legs, or two, or any one of the four, and the whole with such ease and certainty that it is necessary to witness the feat to have a just conception of the skill displayed.

To acquire such skills, of course, took half a lifetime of practice. Basil Hall noted that lassoing was

the earliest amusement of these people, and I have

Vaqueros breaking in wild horses.

often seen little boys just beginning to run about, actively employed in lassoing cats, and entangling the legs of every dog that was unfortunate enough to pass within reach.

The cowboy's way of life developed out of that of the vaquero. A vaquero never walked if he could ride. He wore his spurs to show that he was a *caballero*, a horseman. The vaquero never faltered in his duty to the herd; he led a dangerous and a lonely life, and, perhaps for that very reason, cherished hospitality, laughter, and friendship all the more. The Abbé Domenech, in a book describing his adventures in Texas and Mexico, has given us a good description of the typical Mexican-American rancher:

When the ranchero is not either resting or amusing himself he mounts his horse and canters over the plains and through the woods to see his herds, to visit his friends, to buy provisions, or assist in a feast, a baptism, a marriage . . . ; but the ranchero never walks. Has he only half a mile to go, he does so on horseback. His horse, of which he is very proud, is his inseparable companion. He is content with a wretched hut for his residence, while he decorates his saddle and bridle with gold and silver ornaments. At home he is all filth; mounted on his horse he wears the gayest attire.

The ranchero tills the soil to some extent, but herds of oxen, horses, goats and sheep make up the bulk of his fortune. This kind of income costs him little labor, and therefore does he like it so much. The pasture lands are rich, fair, and numerous; and the cattle roam over them at large.

*Drawing of a cowboy "indulging in revolver
practice," from Frank Leslie's Illustrated
Newspaper, January 29, 1881.*

The Anglo-Americans adopted Mexican equipment, dress, and ranching methods. Many of the cowboy's terms too, were Mexican. *Corral, remuda, bronco, loco, sombrero,* were copied outright. Other Spanish words became corrupted because of the Texan's inability to pronounce them clearly. Lariat came from *la reata,* the rope; rodeo from *rodear,* to surround with; pinto from *pinta,* a paint horse; lasso from *laso,* a slip knot or loop; chaps from *chaparreras,* leg armor; cinch from *cincha,* girth; ranch from *ranchero;* hoosegow from *jugado,* the prisoner's dock in a Mexican court; and stampede from *stampida,* meaning a crash or loud noise.

In 1836 the Texans made a revolution to win their independence from Mexico; many Mexicans were forced to abandon their herds and homes, and flee south. Anglos rounded up the abandoned cattle and began to build up their herds. Some of them raided Mexican ranches, drove off the vaqueros and captured the cattle. These Texans were called "cowboys," and for many years the name was not considered a good one to have.

Between 1840 and 1860 the ranching industry in Texas began to expand in response to developing opportunities in North American markets. Steamboats carried cattle to New Orleans and overland drives were made to other Mississippi River ports. The sturdy Longhorns, some 200,000 of them, it is estimated, were driven over the Shawnee trail into Missouri in the twenty years preceding the Civil War.

In 1852 two young Illinoisians, Washington Malone and Tom Candy Ponting, made the trip to Texas and bought cattle which they drove back to Illinois. They selected 130 of the best steers, shipped them by train to New Jersey, and then ferried them across the Hudson River to New York. These steers were the first Longhorns ever to reach New York City. The two partners sold them on July 4, 1854, for a good profit, and the *New York Tribune* made the following comment:

This drove started in April, 1853, and drove four months to Illinois, where they were watered, and then drove to Marius, Indiana, and thence by cars to Cleveland, Erie, Dunkirk and by way of the Erie road. This made about 1,500 on foot and 600 miles on the railroad. The expense from Texas to Illinois was about $2 a head, the owners camping out all the way. From Illinois here the expense is about $17 a head. The drove came 500 miles through the Indian country . . . part of the route was through the Kansas Territory.

The top of the drove are good quality of beef, and all are fair. These cattle are generally 5, 6, and 7 years old, rather long-legged, though fine-horned, with long tapir horns, and something of a wild look.

In the 1850's there were several outbreaks of Spanish or Texas fever in Missouri and Kansas. The disease was due to ticks carried by the Longhorns up the trail. The hardy Texas cattle were not affected by the ticks; they were merely carriers of the disease which passed to domestic cattle on the route. At the Kansas and Missouri borders mobs of armed farmers met the Texas herds and turned them back; many states passed quarantine laws designed to keep the Texas cattle out. When the Civil War broke out the drives ceased entirely, and the

Rounding up Longhorns.

Shawnee road became an empty highway. The ranchers and drivers joined the Confederate Army and rode off to fight the Yankees.

During the war the cattle were neglected, wandered away, and became wild. Prices fell to almost nothing and beef became practically a forgotten food. Texas did not suffer the devastation that other Southern states did during the conflict, but life was hard. George W. Saunders, who later became a prosperous rancher, wrote about one of these drives:

We were happy and prosperous until the Civil War started. Father and my eldest brother entered the service the first year, and another brother enlisted the second year, which left brother Jack and myself to take care of our stock with the assistance of a few old men and some Negroes. George Bell, who was exempt from military service on account of one eye being blind, agreed to take a herd of beeves to Mexico and exchange them for supplies for the war widows. The neighbors got together about two hundred of these beeves, my mother putting in twenty head.

How little cattle were then worth is shown by Saunders' list of the items which George Bell accepted in return for these twenty head of Saunders family cattle:

When he returned from Mexico he brought us one sack of coffee, two sets of knives and forks, two pairs of spurs, two bridle bits, and two fancy "hackamores," or bridle headstalls. . . . We were well pleased with our deal, for in those days such things were considered luxuries, and we were glad to get them, particularly the knives and forks, for we had been drinking bran coffee and were using wooden knives and forks we had made ourselves. Those were hard times in Goliad County during the Civil War.

At the close of the war, Texans, like most other Southerners, were living in poverty. Ranches were run down and facing ruin. Confederate money was worthless. The one asset, of course, that Texas had was its cattle—millions of them, with many, perhaps one third or one quarter of the total, running wild and unbranded. People called themselves "cattle poor," and measured their poverty by the number of cattle that they possessed.

The problem for the Texans was how to get all these wild cattle to a paying market. During the Civil War the northern economy had undergone a gigantic expansion. In the period following the war huge quantities of meat would be needed to feed the millions of industrial workers and new immigrants flocking to America's mines, mills, and factories. But Mississippi steamboats could not carry many cattle north, and railroads had not yet been driven out to Texas.

The nearest railroad depots were to the north, in Missouri and Kansas. In 1866, accordingly, Texans began to round up their cattle and drive them north on foot. Their objective was Sedalia, Missouri. In the spring and early summer of that year about one quarter of a million cattle crossed the Red River and headed into Indian Territory.

The drivers ran into nothing but trouble. The Indians demanded payment of ten cents a head for the grass the

Longhorns would eat in passing through their land. Missouri and Kansas farmers, remembering the terrible effects of the Spanish fever, swarmed out with rifles in hand to stop the herds.

Even worse was the menace of armed ruffians whom the Texans called Jayhawkers. These Jayhawkers threatened to stampede the herds if they were not paid off. Outnumbered, the Texans often had either to pay or to give the outlaws part of their herds. Some fought back; many a cowboy died defending his cattle from Jayhawker attacks.

A young trail driver, James M. Daugherty, told about his reception after having crossed the border into Kansas:

Some twenty miles south of Fort Scott, Kansas, and about four o'clock one afternoon, a bunch of fifteen or twenty Jayhawkers came upon us. One of my cowboys, John Dobbins by name, was leading the herd, and I was riding close to the leader. Upon approach of the Jayhawkers John attempted to draw his gun and the Jayhawkers shot him dead in the saddle. This caused the cattle to stampede and at the same time they covered me with their guns and I was forced to surrender. The rest of the cowboys stayed with the herd, losing part of them in the stampede. The Jayhawkers took me to Cow Creek which was near by, and there tried me for driving cattle into their country, which [cattle] they claimed were infested with ticks which would kill their cattle. I was found guilty without any evidence, they not even having one of my cattle for evidence.

Daugherty came off with his life, and in this was

luckier than his friend John Dobbins. "They began," he went on,

> to argue among themselves what to do with me. Some wanted to hang me while others wanted to whip me to death. I, being a young man in my teens, and my sympathetic talk about being ignorant of tickey cattle at the south diseasing any of the cattle in their country, caused one of the big Jayhawkers to take my part. The balance was strong for hanging me on the spot, but through his arguments they finally let me go. After I was freed and had joined the herd, two of my cowboys and I slipped back and buried John Dobbins where he fell.

As a result of harassment such as this, many herds were turned back, while others reached market thin and undernourished. For most of the trail drivers the year 1866 was a total loss, and only 35,000 cattle reached the railheads. As one writer put it, "All the bright prospects of marketing, profitably, the immense livestock of Texas faded away, or worse, proved to those who tried driving, a serious financial loss. Never, perhaps, in the history of Texas, was the business of cattle ranching at so low estate as about the close of the year 1866."

Down by the Brazos

Lie li lie lee lee lee give me your hand,
lie li lie lee lee lee give me your hand,
Lie li lie lee lee lee give me your hand, There's
ma - ny a riv - er that wat - ers the land. We

Lie li lie lee lee lee, give me your hand,
Lie li lie lee lee lee, give me your hand,
Lie li lie lee lee lee, give me your hand,
There's many a river that waters the land.

We crossed the broad Pecos, we forded the Nueces,
We swum the Guadaloupe, we forded the Brazos,
Red River runs rusty, the Wichita clear,
But down by the Brazos I courted my dear.

REFRAIN

The fair Angelina runs glossy and gliding,
The crooked Colorado runs weaving and winding,
The broad San Antonio courses the plain,
But I never will walk by the Brazos again.

REFRAIN

She hugged me, she kissed me, she called me her dandy,
The Trinity's muddy, the Brazos quicksandy,
She hugged me, she kissed me, she called me her own,
But down by the Brazos she left me alone.

REFRAIN

The girls of New River are plump and they're pretty,
The Sabine and the Sulphur have many a beauty,
On the banks of the Natchez there's girls by the score,
But down by the Brazos I'll wander no more.

3

ABILENE AND THE CHISHOLM TRAIL

Where could the Texans turn? By 1867 six states—
Colorado, Nebraska, Kansas, Missouri, Illinois and Ken-
tucky—barred Longhorns. But the Kansas law did offer
a possible loophole, for Texas cattle could still be driven
into the western part of the state where farmers had not
yet settled. The Kansas Pacific railroad was pushing
westward across Kansas. If the herds could reach one of
its railheads the cattle could be loaded up and shipped
back East; tremendous profits might then be made from
the sale of beef to the swarming wage earners of the
industrial towns.

Texas had the cattle, the northern feeders and packers
had the money, the railroads offered a means of transportation. Could all three get together?

A young man from Illinois, Joseph G. McCoy, had the
vision, energy, and enthusiasm to set things in motion.
Born December 21, 1837, the youngest of nine children,
McCoy had gone into the livestock and shipping business with two of his brothers. He first became aware of
the problems of Texas herders when he bought W. W.
Sugg's herd in the spring of 1867. Sugg was an Illinois

cattle dealer who had gone down to Texas and had purchased steers to drive back north. McCoy now moved into action to enlarge the flow of cattle from the south. In his own account, *Historic Sketches of the Cattle Trade,* McCoy tells his story in the third person:

This young man conceived the idea of opening up an outlet for Texan cattle. Being impressed with a knowledge of the number of cattle in Texas and the difficulties of getting them to market by the routes and means then in use, and realizing the great disparity of Texas values and Northern prices of cattle, he set himself to thinking and studying to hit upon some plan whereby these great extremes would be equalized. It was to establish a market whereat the Southern drover and Northern buyer would meet upon an equal footing, and both be undisturbed by mobs or swindling thieves. The longer the idea of this enterprise was harbored by the young Illinois cattle shipper, the more determined he became and the more enthusiastic to carry it out.

McCoy decided that this market should be located on the prairie along the route of the Kansas Pacific. He visited Junction City and tried to buy land there to build a stockyard and other facilities, but the owner of the property refused to sell at any price. McCoy was undiscouraged, and started to look for another shipping point where he could build his market. But first of all he called upon the President of the Missouri Pacific railroad at St. Louis. This was necessary because the Kansas Pacific ran no further than the eastern boarder of Kansas. What freight charges would he have to pay on the

Joseph G. McCoy.

Missouri Pacific that would take the cattle from eastern Kansas into St. Louis? Here is McCoy's account of his interview with the railroad magnate:

Here was the first really great man engaged in the contemptible occupation of managing a railroad, that the Illinoisan ever beheld. Entering the elegant office of the President . . . he timidly stated his business in modest terms, and asked what rates of freight would be charged on the stock coming to St. Louis. . . . The railroad official, tipping his cigar up at right angles to his nose, and striking an attitude of indescribable greatness, . . . and with an air bordering on immensity, said: "It occurs to me that you haven't any cattle to ship and never did have any, and I, sir, have no evidence that you ever will have any, and I think you are talking about rates of freight for speculative purposes, therefore you get out of this office, and let me not be troubled with any more of your style."

So McCoy left the office, and arranged to ship his cattle to Chicago instead. In this casual fashion St. Louis lost the chance of becoming the country's greatest meat and packing center.

McCoy now turned back to the task of selecting a railhead in Kansas from which the Texas cattle might be shipped. He settled finally upon Abilene, the seat of Dickinson county, and a scrubby frontier village not more than six years old.

Abilene in 1867 was a very small, dead place, consisting of about one dozen log huts, low, small, rude affairs, four-fifths of which were covered with dirt for roofing;

The Railroad King and the Illinoisan.

indeed but one shingle roof could be seen in the whole city. The business of the burg was conducted in two small rooms, mere log huts, and of course, the inevitable saloon, also a log hut, was to be found.

Abilene lay in Smoky Hill Valley which possessed wide meadows and rich grass. McCoy selected it

because the country was entirely unsettled, well watered, had excellent grass, and nearly the entire area of the country was adapted to holding cattle.

In making his choice McCoy was, as a matter of fact, violating the Kansas Quarantine Law. But the lands around Abilene were at the time thinly settled. Nobody, at least at first, protested the town's being chosen as a center for Texas cattle.

McCoy set to work to build his stockyards, and sent Sugg down the trail to Texas with instructions to contact as many cattlemen as he could and to tell them about the facilities awaiting them in Abilene.

This was joyous news to the drover, for the fear of trouble and violence hung like an incubus over his waking thoughts alike with his sleeping moments . . . could it be possible that someone was about to afford a Texan drover any other reception than outrage and robbery? They were very suspicious that some trap was set, to be sprung on them; they were not ready to credit the proposition that the day of fair dealing had dawned for Texan drovers, and the era of mobs, brutal murder, and arbitrary proscription ended forever. Yet they turned their herds toward the point designated, and slowly and cautiously moved on northward. . . .

Stockyards on the Kansas Pacific Railroad.

Not more than 35,000 cattle arrived at Abilene in 1867. But this marked the beginning of a new era in the history of the west and the start of the famous Chisholm Trail. McCoy tells how the first shipment of cattle from Abilene to Chicago took place on September 5:

Several Illinois stockmen and others joined in an excursion from Springfield, Illinois, to Abilene to celebrate by feast, wine and song, the auspicious event. Arriving at Abilene in the evening [they found] several large tents, including one for dining purposes, ready for the reception of guests. A substantial repast was spread before the excursionists, . . . after which wine, toasts and speechifying were the order until a late hour at night. Before the sun had mounted high in the heavens on the following day, the iron horse was darting down the Kaw Valley with the first train load of cattle that ever passed over the Kansas Pacific Railroad, the precursor to many thousands to follow.

Altogether in 1867, almost 1,000 carloads of cattle were shipped from Abilene over the Hannibal and St. Joe Railroad to packing plants in Chicago. The Texans received half a million Yankee dollars for their stock. This money, carried back to Texas, spread the message of Abilene, the cattle town for Texan Longhorns, far and wide.

The Chisholm Trail, upon which Texas cattle would now travel to Abilene, lay 150 miles west of the old Shawnee Trail; it followed a track that had been used by buffalo and Indians for countless years back. The trail was named after Jesse Chisholm, who had used it as a wagon route for his trade with the Indians. It was, of

course, only one of several great trails that the Texas cattle would follow on their trek north. But it remained the most famous.

In 1868, 75,000 cattle reached Abilene, and most of these were shipped east—so many, indeed, that the railroad was unable to provide enough cars for their passage. Abilene as a cattle market, wrote McCoy, "was at last

Shipping Longhorns on the Kansas Pacific, from Frank Leslie's Illustrated Newspaper, August 19, 1871.

established beyond cavil or doubt." Gleefully now, McCoy took his revenge upon the pompous president of the Missouri Pacific:

Now, when . . . shipments began to go forward at a lively rate, and any man, although a fool, could see the success of the enterprise, an agent of the Missouri Pacific

Road put in an appearance at Abilene and was very solicitous for business for his road. But the memory of the insulting conduct of his official superior was still fresh in the mind of the Illinoisan, and he told the agent that "it occurred to him that he had no cattle for his road, never had had and there was no evidence that he ever would have, and please to say so to his President."

As the Longhorns flocked to Abilene, McCoy held auctions at two-week intervals and sold them off. The *Weekly Union* reported on July 25, 1868, that at the first auction "five hundred head were disposed of. The large work cattle averaged thirty dollars per head, the two-year-olds, ten dollars per head. A large number of bidders were present from four states."

But Abilene was still unknown to most cattle buyers and Eastern investors. So McCoy took further steps to advertise his depot and its wares. He decided to send East a carload of buffalo, covering the sides of the car with advertisements for cattle.

Four Texas cowboys and two Californian vaqueros were hired to ride out upon the prairie and capture the needed buffalo. The task was not a simple one. A. M. Withers, one of these cowboys, told about it in *Trail Drivers of Texas:*

In about a week we captured twenty-four buffalo bulls. Some of them died from heat and anger caused by capture, others became sullen and laid down before they were gotten near the cars, and only twelve were successfully loaded and started on the road to Chicago.

After hanging upon each side of the cars an advertise-

ment of the cattle near Abilene, they were sent to Chicago via St. Louis, causing much newspaper comment. Upon reaching Chicago the buffalo were sent to the Fair Grounds, where the two Spaniards, Billy Campbell and I roped them again to show the people how it was done. This advertisement feat was followed by an excursion of Illinois cattle men to the West. The people were taken to the prairies near Abilene and shown the many fine herds of cattle. Several people invested in these cattle, and in a short time the market at Abilene assumed its usual life and activity. The year of 1868 closed with Abilene's success as a cattle market of note. Soon Texas cattle became in great demand for packing.

In the following years, railroads, investors, and meat companies made money out of the cattle business. McCoy himself along with his brothers suffered heavy financial losses and was forced into bankruptcy. He ended up with little to show for his efforts except a nervous breakdown. The Kansas Pacific Railroad refused to honor the contract they had signed with him, denying that they had promised to pay McCoy a share of the profits taken on each carload of cattle shipped. Though he sued the railroad and finally won a ruling in his favor, it was an empty victory.

So after a two-year struggle, the Railway Company paid the amount originally claimed, and for the lack of which the Illinoisan had been bankrupted. All the bright assurance and promises given him in the beginning by the Railway Executive Committee, through its President, thus terminated, and poverty in abundance was given where emoluments had been promised.

Beef processing plant in Kansas City, Missouri.

True, he obtained the amount of the judgment less expenses and attorney's fees, but it lacked only twelve days of being two years after it was due; in which time his business had gone to ruin, and losses were entailed him of many thousands of dollars.

But the industry that McCoy had helped to found went on. Prices for beef were good; profits were to be made by almost all concerned, especially cattlemen, railroads, and buyers. The western territories were filling up with settlers who needed cattle to stock their farms; beef was supplanting pork as the mainstay of the American workingman's table; miners in the western camps, construction and maintenance crews on the railroads, all needed beef and were willing to pay the price. The Federal Government itself needed large supplies to feed the Indians whom it sent to the reservations, and the soldiers who drove them there.

1871 was a banner year. More than 600,000 head of cattle went up the trail, twice as many as in 1870; Kansas was filled to bursting with Longhorns, and it seemed as though all Texas was on the move. The Salina *County Journal* reported, July 20, 1871:

The entire country east, west, and south of Salina down to the Arkansas River and Wichita is now filled with Texas cattle. There are not only "cattle on a thousand hills" but a thousand cattle on one hill and every hill. The bottoms are overflowing with them and the water courses with this great article of traffic. Perhaps not less than 200,000 head are in the State, 60,000 of which are within a day's ride of Salina, and the cry is "still they come!"

Abilene's prosperity was short-lived. Many townsmen objected to the vice and crime that came along with the drives. Farmers settled in great numbers on the prairie around the town. They disliked the wild Longhorns who knocked down their fences and trampled their crops. In February, 1872, the following notice appeared in the local paper, *The Chronicle:*

We, the undersigned, members of the Farmers' Protective Association, and officers and citizens of Dickinson County, Kansas, most respectfully request all who have contemplated driving Texas cattle to Abilene the coming season, to seek some other point for shipment, as the inhabitants of Dickinson will no longer submit to the evils of that trade.

Other towns and railheads, seeing Abilene's prosperity, attempted to capture a share of the cattle trade. Salina, Ellsworth, Newton, Wichita, and Dodge City all entered into the competition. There were so many herds that there was enough business for all. Each town had its moment of fame or notoriety as the trails bent ever westward across the unsettled prairies.

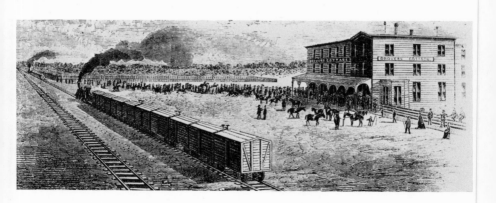

Colorado Trail

Guitar instrumental

Eyes like the mor-ning star, Cheeks like a rose,

Laur-a was a pret-ty girl, God al-might-y knows.

Weep, all ye lit-tle rains, Wail, winds, wail,

All a - long, a - long, a - long the Col- o - ra- do Trail.

Eyes like the morning star,
Cheeks like a rose,
Laura was a pretty girl,
God almighty knows;
Weep all ye little rains
Wail, winds, wail;
All along, along, along
The Colorado Trail.

Ride through the stormy night,
Dark is the sky,
Wish I'd stayed in Abilene,
Nice and warm and dry;
Weep all ye little rains,
Wail, winds, wail;
All along, along, along
The Colorado Trail

UP THE TRAIL

The trail experience has been vividly recorded for us in a Western classic by Andy Adams, entitled *The Log of a Cowboy*. Adams was an Indiana farm boy whose family moved to Texas after the Civil War. His two older brothers became cowboys, and Andy was eager to follow in their footsteps. "The fascination of a horse and saddle," he wrote, "was too strong to be resisted." By the time he was sixteen he took to the range "as a preacher's son takes to vice."

In 1882, at the age of eighteen, Andy was engaged by Jim Flood, foreman for the Texan drover Don Lovell. The assignment was to drive a herd of cattle all the way from the Rio Grande to the Blackfoot Indian Reservation in northwestern Montana. This was in fulfillment of a contract that Lovell had with the Federal Government to provide cattle to feed the Indians.

Andy left home one day in March to join his outfit.

My worst trouble was getting away from home on the morning of starting. Mother and my sisters, of course, shed a few tears; but my father, stern and unbending in his manner, gave me his benediction in these words: "You are the third son to have left our roof, but your father's blessing goes with you."

As the family stood by the farm gate, Andy climbed into his saddle and rode away "with a lump in my throat which left me speechless to reply."

Down by the Rio Grande, Andy heard Don Lovell give last minute instructions to Flood, who was to be the trail boss:

Now, Jim, I can't give you any pointers on handling a herd, but you have until the 10th day of September to reach the Blackfoot Agency. An average of fifteen miles a day will put you there on time, so don't hurry. I'll try and see you at Dodge and Ogallala on the way. Now live well, for I like your outfit of men. Your credit letter is good anywhere you need supplies; and if you want more horses on the trail, buy them and draft on me through your letter of credit. If any of your men meet with accident or get sick, look out for them, the same as you would for yourself and I'll honor all bills. And don't be stingy over your expense account, for if that herd doesn't make money, you and I had better quit now.

The first week on the trail was the crucial one. Cattle were strongly attached to their home range and did not like to leave it. If the herd could be properly broken to the road they would be much easier to drive the rest of the way. There would be less danger of the hazard that cowboys dreaded most—the stampede or "run." The herd that Andy was with was called the Circle Dot.

Flood assured his men that they were doing a good job in road-breaking the Circle Dot:

This herd is breaking into trail life nicely. If we'll just be careful with them now for the first month and no bad storms strike us in the night, we may never have a run the entire trip. That last drink of water they had this evening gave them a night-cap that'll last them until morning. No, there's no danger of any trouble tonight.

Usually only the ablest and most experienced men were taken along on the trail. An average trail crew consisted of a trail boss, a cook, a horse wrangler and eight to eighteen cowboys, depending upon the size of the herd. 1,000 to 3,000 Longhorns made up a herd; more than that was unwieldy.

The cowboys took up a certain pattern and order on the trail. The trail boss rode out ahead and surveyed the route. Then he signaled his point men the direction in which they were to go. The whole movement of the herd was directed by such signals, learned from the Indians.

Adams described the moving herd:

On the morning of April 1, 1882, our Circle Dot herd started on its long tramp. With six men on each side, and the herd strung out for three quarters of a mile, it could only be compared with some mystical serpent or Chinese dragon as it moved forward on its sinuous, snail-like course. Two riders, known as point men, rode out and well back from the lead cattle; and, by riding forward and closing in as occasion required, directed the course of the herd. The main body of the herd trailed along behind the leaders, like an army in loose marching order, guarded by outriders, known as swing men, who rode well out from the advancing column, warding off range cattle and seeing that none of the herd wandered away or dropped out.

The cattle were allowed to move in a free and leisurely fashion, and were not bunched up. The Longhorns were expected to gain weight as they moved along the trail and to arrive at the market in good condition. As Flood told his crew:

Boys, the secret of trailing cattle is never to let the herd know that they are under restraint. Let everything that is done be done voluntarily by the cattle. From the moment that you let them off the bed ground in the morning until they are bedded down at night never let a cow take a step except in the direction of its destination. In this manner you can loaf away the day, and cover from fifteen to twenty miles, and the herd in the meantime will enjoy all the freedom of an open range. Of course, it's long and tiresome hours to the men, but the condition of the herd and saddle stock demand sacrifices on our part.

The Longhorns, too, had their fixed positions on the trail, and usually kept them for the whole trip. Day after day they were found in the same position with their own traveling companions. The cowboys got to know most of the steers and were able to tell one from another by sight. The stronger and faster ones took their places in the front, and the cowboys came to depend upon them to lead the herd and keep it moving. If a steer became footsore it dropped back; once better, it moved up to its rightful place again. This regularity in the line of march helped the cowpunchers to keep a check on their charges and to know when one or more was missing.

The tail end of the herd was called a "drag" and never was a truer term coined. Here clustered the cripples, the worn-outs, the sullen, and the lazy, to be pushed along by the "drag men." Drag men had the dirtiest and hardest job. Dust from four to eight thousand hoofs blew in their faces, choking and stinging them. The sun was hot, water was scarce, and the men might go for seven or eight hours without a drink. Men were assigned to the drag because they were the least experienced—or because the trail boss wanted to punish them. The drag was a good place to learn cuss words.

The cowboy's day was from dawn to sunset, and added to this were at least two hours of night duty. In emergencies, of course, like storms or stampedes, he would be up the entire night. It was an axiom of the range that a trail hand was supposed to get his sleep in the winter.

At the first streak of dawn the camp was astir, and the men rolled out of their blankets to the cook's cry of "Day's a-breaking, come and git it!" Cowboys dressed simply by putting on their hats and pulling on their trousers and boots; washing was usually postponed until the sun came up. Hot coffee, gulped black, washed down a hurried breakfast. Bedding was rolled up and placed near the chuck wagon. The men then saddled their horses and mounted them.

Breakfast dishes were washed and the wrangler helped the cook load the wagon and hitch up his horses or mules. The trail boss gave the signal to break camp and

Cowboys on the trail in Wyoming, about 1890.

the pointers started moving the lead cattle along, with the rest of the herd drifting slowly behind. After two or three hours the cattle were moved along a little more briskly until about an hour before noon, when the trail boss gave the signal to make camp.

The Longhorns were then watered, if water was available, and allowed to graze alongside the trail and rest during the hottest hours of the day. The cook, who had made camp ahead of the others, had a meal waiting. Half the cowboys came in, ate hurriedly, changed their horses, and went back to the herd. Then the other half of the men came in to eat.

In late afternoon the herd was driven onto the trail again. The cattle were thirsty, and easier to move along as they were anxious to reach water. If all went well they reached a new campsite before sundown. The boss tried to choose a flat, open spot with fresh grass and water nearby. This site was called the bedground.

At the bedground the cook prepared the main meal of the day; the tired, hungry, thirsty men ate supper. Then they saddled up the night ponies and those with first guard shift went on duty; the others were free to relax for the first time that day. Andy tells how he and his buddy, Priest, prepared for bed:

Priest and I picketed our horses, saddled where we could easily find them in the darkness, and unrolled our bed. We had two pairs of blankets each, which, with an ordinary wagon sheet doubled up for a tarpaulin, and coats and boots for pillows, completed our couch. We slept otherwise in our clothing worn during the day; and if smooth, sandy ground was available on which to spread our bed, we had no trouble in sleeping the sleep that long hours in the saddle were certain to bring.

As darkness fell, the cattle, too, sank to their knees and bedded down for sleep. During the night they had to be constantly watched. The hours from eight until dawn were divided into four two-hour shifts, with each puncher taking his turn. Men slept with or near their partners so that night riders coming off duty knew where to find them. They never woke a cowboy by touching him, but first called his name, and spoke to him. A man awakened too suddenly might come up shooting; Indians, rustlers, and outlaws were common dangers on the trail.

Speaking of night duty, Adams writes:

The guards ride in a circle about four rods outside the sleeping cattle; and by riding in opposite directions make it impossible for any animal to make its escape without being noticed by the riders. The guards usually sing or whistle continuously, so that the sleeping herd may know that a friend and not an enemy is keeping vigil over their dreams.

One of the most beautiful of the many lullabies sung to the cattle was "The Night Herding Song."

The Night Herding Song

(See Acknowledgments, page 191)

Oh, slow up, dog-ies, quit mov-ing a-round, You have wan-dered and tram-pled all o-ver the ground; Oh graze a-long, dog-ies, and feed kind-a slow, And don't for-ev-er be on the go, Move

slow, lit - tle dog - ies, move slow, _____ Hi -

o, Hi - o, _____ Hi - o. _____

Oh, slow up dogies, quit moving around,
You have wandered and trampled all over the ground;
Oh, graze along dogies and feed kinda slow,
And don't forever be on the go.
Move slow little dogies, move slow,
Hi-o, hi-o, hi-o.

Oh say, little dogies, when you goin' to lay down,
And give up this driftin' and rovin' around?
My horse is leg-weary and I'm awful tired,
But if you get away, I'm sure to be fired.
Lay down, little dogies, lay down,
Hi-o, hi-o, hi-o.

Oh, lay still, dogies, since you have laid down,
Stretch away out on the big open ground;
Snore loud, little dogies, and drown the wild sounds,
That'll go away when the day rolls around.
Lay still, little dogies, lay still,
Hi-o, hi-o, hi-o.

Stampede was the thing cowboys dreaded most. Long-horns were nervous animals, easily frightened, and any-thing that scared one Longhorn could start the whole herd running. "The cattle," wrote Adams,

might be lying on the ground in quiet, and apparently intending to stay there in peace til morning. Suddenly one common impulse brought them to their feet and started them on a wild, headlong rush through the dark-ness. Away they went in a frantic, stumbling, panic-crazy plunging mass with little bluish flames flickering at the tips of their horns—electric lights caused by the friction of their hairy bodies in the jam.

Causes for a stampede could vary from the striking of a match to a horse shaking itself, or from a tumbleweed suddenly blown into the herd, or the flapping of a cow-boy's slicker. The most common cause was storm accom-panied by thunder and lightning. The cattle became rest-less and nervous before a storm. The night riders rode around slowly, crooning to the cattle and trying to drown out the whistling of the wind, the muttering and rum-bling in the clouds.

As the cattle started running, it was the job of the herders to stay with them. At the first sound of a stam-pede the sleeping cowboys leaped up, mounted their horses, and galloped after the herd. The punchers gave free rein to their steeds, whose eyesight and instinct were better and surer than their own. The whole ground trem-bled. The rampaging cattle gave off an overpowering smell, as well as a heat so intense that it might blister the faces of men riding alongside.

Stampedes were costly, in both men and cattle. Steers

"The Stampede," a painting by John Henrici.

were scattered over a huge area; the cowboys had to roam the countryside to round them up. Some were never found. Others were crushed to death where they stumbled and fell, ran over bluffs, or leaped from river-banks and drowned. Many who were crippled or badly hurt had to be shot.

When dawn broke after a night stampede, the men checked to see if all their comrades were accounted for. After a long search of the prairies, coulees, and gulches, a missing man might be found thrown from his horse or at the foot of a precipice. But there were other hazards more dangerous to the cowboy than stampedes. Many a tragedy was caused by lightning; when in camp, cowboys took off their spurs, six-shooters, and other metal objects, put them on the ground, and moved away. A. B. Withers of Lockhart, Texas, was an eyewitness to one such tragedy:

While I was delivering cattle to Gus Johnson, he was killed by lightning. G. B. Withers, Johnson and I were riding together when lightning struck. It set Johnson's undershirt on fire and his gold shirt stud, which was set with a diamond, was melted and the diamond never found. His hat was torn to pieces and mine had all the plush burned off the top. I was not seriously hurt, but G. B. Withers lost one eye by the same stroke that killed Johnson.

As the trails moved northward they intersected river after river flowing from west to east. Men, horses, and cattle had to ford these rivers, or, if there was no ford and the water was deep, swim across. But crossing any river was a difficult job. Cattle were as easily frightened in the water as on land. A sudden wave, a floating tree, or a loud noise might throw them into panic. The lead animals would stop and try to turn back. Hundreds of animals would mill around, become exhausted, and be swept downstream to their doom.

If the cowboys hoped to save the cattle they had to plunge into the mill at once and break it up. Turning their swimming horses into the tangle of horns and kicking hooves, they struck at the steers, yelling and cursing, trying to make them head for the bank. Many a man was lost in these melees; his body, swept off by the current, was never found. Adams recounts just such an incident when a member of his outfit, Wade Scholar, was lost:

Amid the general hilarity, I recognized a shout that was born of fear and terror. A hushed silence fell upon the riotous riders in the river and I saw those on the sandbar rush down the narrow island and plunge back into the middle channel. Then it dawned on my mind in a flash that someone had lost his seat, and that terrified cry was for help. I plunged my gray into the river. There were not less than twenty horsemen drifting in the middle channel in the hope that whoever it was would come to the surface, and a hand could be stretched out in succor.

In the early spring and the fall, the streams were constantly swollen by rain. But during the summer the cowboys had to meet an opposite problem—a lack of water for animals and men. Then the sun burned down from a cloudless sky onto a land where there were no trees, no shade. The cowboys' lips became cracked and dried.

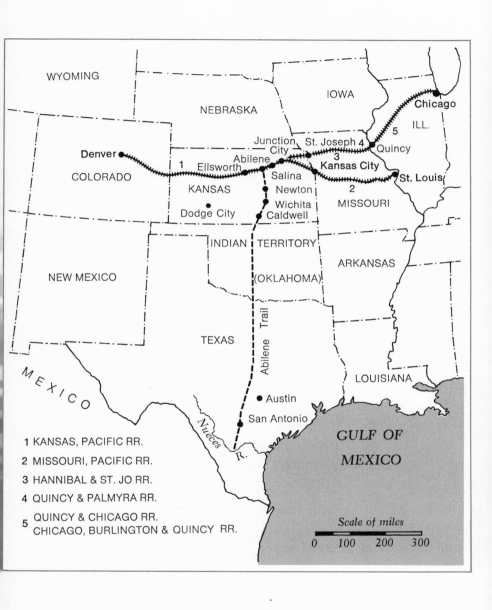

WYOMING

NEBRASKA

IOWA

Chicago

ILL.

Denver

COLORADO

Junction City
St. Joseph 4
Abilene
Ellsworth
1
Salina
KANSAS
Newton
Dodge City
Wichita
Caldwell

Quincy

Kansas City

St. Louis

2

MISSOURI

NEW MEXICO

INDIAN TERRITORY

(OKLAHOMA)

ARKANSAS

TEXAS

Abilene Trail

LOUISIANA

MEXICO

Nueces R.

Austin

San Antonio

GULF OF

MEXICO

1 KANSAS, PACIFIC RR.

2 MISSOURI, PACIFIC RR.

3 HANNIBAL & ST. JO RR.

4 QUINCY & PALMYRA RR.

5 QUINCY & CHICAGO RR.
   CHICAGO, BURLINGTON & QUINCY RR.

Scale of miles

0   100   200   300

The steers' tongues hung out, swelled up, and turned black. An alkali dust hung in the air and the punchers were coated with it from head to foot. It got into their mouths and down into their lungs.

Trail drivers frequently met Indians upon the trail. Indians might assault outriders or isolated men looking for strays. Sometimes they stampeded the herds at night and then rounded up scattered cattle for food. Not infrequently, hungry Indians begged a steer or two from the cowboys. Adams tells about one such encounter:

Flood opened the pow-wow by demanding to know the meaning of this visit. When the question had been properly interpreted to the chief, the latter dropped his blanket from his shoulders and dismounted from his horse. He was a fine specimen of the Plains Indian, fully six feet in height, perfectly proportioned, and in years well past middle life. He looked every inch a chief, and was a natural born orator. There was a certain grace to his gestures, only to be seen in people who use the sign language. . . .

Before the pow-wow had progressed far, it was evident that begging was its object. In his prelude, the chief laid claims to all the country in sight as the hunting grounds of the Comanche tribe—an intimation that we were intruders. He spoke of the great slaughter of the buffalo by the white hide hunters and the consequent hunger and poverty amongst his people. He dwelt on the fact that he had ever counciled peace with the whites, until now his band numbered but a few squaws and papooses, the younger men having deserted him for other chiefs of the tribe who advocated war on the palefaces. . . . He offered to allow us to pass through his country in consideration of ten beeves.

The outcome of the negotiations that followed was that Jim Flood gave the Indians three beeves and the Indians allowed the herd to continue up the trail. Sometimes the Indians were even more helpful. They assisted in swimming the herds across the rivers or pulling horses free from quicksands.

White rustlers and renegades were more of a problem. These outlaws sometimes disguised themselves as Indians in order to cast the blame for their crimes upon others. They attacked the cowboys, stampeded the cattle, and drove off the stock. They robbed returning trailmen of the gold or other currency they had received for the sale of their herds at the railheads.

The drive from Texas to Abilene took from two to four months, and from Texas to Montana or the Dakotas, up to six months. As these trips wore on, the men became more and more fatigued. Conversations became rare. But finally there came a day when the point man heard a new sound or saw a new sight. He would rein in to look or listen more carefully. Perhaps it was the crowing of a rooster or the roof of a house. As the word passed down the line, the atmosphere would change as men began to smile, joke and talk. Fatigue seemed to fall away, they sat up straighter in the saddle and rode easier, and even the cattle seemed to move along in a more lively way. Civilization and the railroad corral lay ahead.

Git Along Little Dogies

Guitar instrumental

As I was a walk-ing one morn-ing for pleas-ure, I spied a cow-pun-cher a rid-ing a-long; His hat was throwed back and his spurs was a-jing-ling,

As he ap - proached me sing - ing this song: Whoo-pee ti yi yo, Git a - long, lit-tle dog - ies! It's your mis-fort - une and none of my own, Whoo-pee ti yi yo, Git a - long lit-tle dog - ies, For you

know   Wy - o - ming   will   be   your   new   home.

As I was a-walking one morning for pleasure,
I spied a cowpuncher a-riding along.
His hat was thrown back and his spurs was a-jingling,
As he approached me singing this song:

REFRAIN:
Whoopee ti yi yo, git along little dogies,
It's your misfortune and none of my own,
Whoopee ti yi yo, git along little dogies,
For you know Montana will be your new home.

Some of the boys goes up the trail for pleasure,
But that's where they git it most awfully wrong;
For you've no idea the trouble they give us
When we go driving them dogies along.

REFRAIN

Oh, you'll be soup for Uncle Sam's Injuns,
"It's beef, heap beef," I hear them cry.
Git along, git along, git along little dogies,
You're going to be beef steers by and by.

REFRAIN

IN TOWN

To Abilene, and then to the other railroad depots, came the cowboys and their beasts. The herds were halted at the edge of town and held for buyers to come out and negotiate; most of the cowboys were paid off. They lost no time riding into town, looking for fun and female company.

Teddy Blue Abbott rode up the Texas trails in the 1870's and 1880's. He was one of the few ranch hands who married the boss' daughter and became a rancher himself. In his autobiography, *We Pointed Them North*, Teddy admitted that cowboys were wild, but explained their behavior as a reaction to the hard and dangerous life they led.

. . . I wasn't looking for fights. I was looking for fun, and that I believe was the case with nine-tenths of them. They were wild and reckless, it is true, and to understand that you would have to know the kind of life they led. They were not like those city fellows with a saloon on every corner. They didn't get to drink very often. They were out there for months on end, on the trail or living in some cow camp, eating bad food, sleeping in

wet clothes, going without everything that means life to a man . . . and when they hit the bright lights of some little cow town, they just went wild.

There had been a time for trail riding with its dangers and its toil. Now was the cowboy's time to relax and whoop it up, to dance and whore with painted women. Spurs jingling, they swaggered from saloon to dancehall, drinking and gambling in order to forget the stampedes and the rustlers, the swimming of swollen rivers, the death of a comrade, and the monotonous, bonebreaking work of the trail.

The cowboys had worked hard for their wages, but money meant nothing to them. Their three or four months' pay could go in one or two nights of drinking, gambling, and whoring. There was a deep similarity between them and the sailor back in port after months at sea. Their time was now; what was the use of taking money back to Texas?

Providing entertainment soon became an important part of a cow town's business. Vice and crime were brought to these towns by the swarms of gamblers, gunmen, saloon keepers, confidence men, robbers, pimps, and prostitutes who swarmed to them from Memphis, Detroit, Chicago, St. Louis, New Orleans, and other American cities. These people came to prey upon the cowhands. During the cattle season 300–400 cowpunchers rode into town daily to spend their wages. This meant that as much as $40,000 was pouring into the town's cash registers each day.

Upon his arrival in town the cowboy headed first for the barber shop. His next step was to go to a dry-goods

In the saloon.

store and buy a suit of clothes. As Andy Adams tells it,

"The first thing I do when we strike the town of Silver Bow," said Bull Fudurham, as he was putting on his last shirt, "is to discard to the skin and get me new togs to the finish. I'll commence on my little pattering feet, which will require fifteen-dollar moccasins, and top off with a seven-dollar brown Stetson. Then with a few drinks under my belt and a rim-fire cigar in my mouth, I'd admire to meet the governor of Montana if convenient."

All decked out in their new finery, the cowhands usually went to the best restaurant in town and ordered eggs, ice cream, and fresh oysters. After their meal they were ready for action. Cowboys were born gamblers, and every kind of card game and game of chance was awaiting them: monte, faro, vingt-et-un, poker, chuck-o-luck, old sledge, the tobacco box, roulette. As Quince Forrest, one of Andy Adams' buddies, put it:

The very first thing I do is to hunt up that gambler in the Long Branch and ask him to take a drink with me —as I took the parting one on him. Then I'll simply set in and win back every dollar I lost there last year. There's something in this northern air that I breathe this morning that tells me that this is my lucky day. You younger kids had better let the games alone and save your money to buy red silk handkerchiefs and soda water and such harmless jimcracks.

The railroad divided Abilene in two. North of the railroad were the Gore hotel, the houses of the townspeople, the church, and the newspaper office. South of it were the saloons, gambling parlors, dance halls, and houses of prostitution, lining Texas Street. By 1871 there were ten saloons in Abilene, among them the Alamo, the Bull's Head, Old Fruit, Lone Star, the Longhorn, and the Trail. The Alamo was the most stylish. Its glass doors admitted customers to a long bar and gambling tables. Mirrors and paintings of naked women decorated its walls. An orchestra played night and day.

Abilene in the summer was always noisy. Its dusty streets were crowded with cowboys, cattle buyers, freighters with their wagons, mule skinners, stage coach drivers, gunmen, merchants, townspeople, women, and children. The shaky wooden sidewalks trembled and rang to the tramp of the cowboys' boots and the jingle of their spurs. There was a continual bawling of cattle, a rumble of horses' hoofs, a sawing and hammering of carpenters throwing up new buildings, and the whistle and clickety-clack of railroad trains. Guns went off night and day as new groups of cowpunchers drifted into town. The sounds of music and laughing and shouting came from the saloons and dance halls along with the shuffling of cards and the rattle of dice.

Seeking the companionship of women, the cowboys flocked to the dancehalls. Joseph McCoy drew a graphic picture:

Few more wild, reckless scenes of abandoned debauchery can be seen on the civilized earth, than a dance hall in full blast in one of the many frontier towns. To say they dance wildly or in an abandoned manner is putting it mildly. . . . The cowboy enters the dance with a particular zest, not stopping to divest himself of his som-

Mrs. Lou Gore, hotelkeeper, Abilene, Kansas.

brero, spurs or pistols, but just as he dismounts off his cow-pony, so he goes into the dance. A more odd, not to say comical sight is not often seen than the dancing cowboy: with the front of his sombrero lifted at an angle of 45°, his huge spurs jangling at every step or motion, his revolvers flapping up and down like a retreating sheep's tail, his eyes lit up with excitement, liquor and lust, he plunges into it and "hoes it down" at a terrible rate in the most approved yet awkward country style, often swinging his partner clear off the floor for an entire circle; then "balance all" with an occasional demonic yell near akin to the war whoop of the savage Indian. All this he does entirely oblivious to the whole world and the rest of mankind.

Prostitutes carried on a lively trade with the lonely cowboys. The red light district was originally located in town, but after repeated protests from "decent women" was moved to the southeastern edge of Abilene. As one cowboy recalled, "They lived in a part of town called McCoy's addition. Believe me, there were certainly lots of them."

Teddy Blue devoted a whole chapter of his book to the cowboys' experiences with prostitutes. They were the only women cowboys associated with; the nature of their work seldom brought them into contact with any others. Often a good relationship grew up between prostitutes and cowboys, who saw the women simply as human beings rather than as objects of scorn. As Teddy Blue put it:

I suppose those things would shock a lot of respectable people. But we wasn't respectable and we didn't pretend to be, which was the only way we was different from some others. I've heard a lot about the double standard, and seen a lot of it, too, and it don't make any sense for the man to get off so easily. If I'd been a woman and done what I done I'd have ended up in a sporting house.

I used to talk to those girls, and they would tell me a lot of stuff, about how they got started, and how in Chicago and those eastern cities they wasn't allowed on the streets, how their clothes would be taken away from them, only what they needed in the house, so it was like being in prison.

They could do as they pleased out here. And they were human, too. They always had money and they would lend it to fellows that were broke. The wagon bosses would come around looking for men in the spring, and when a fellow was hired he would go to his girl and say: "I've got a job, but my bed's in soak." Or his saddle or his six-shooter or his horse. And she would lend him the money to get it back and he would pay her at the end of the month.

The Texans came into town ready to blow off steam and spend their money; many of them stayed only three or four days before leaving, broke and busted. The townsfolk found it hard to understand their exuberance. To them, all Texans seemed the same—wild, desperate characters ready to shoot at the drop of a hat.

Texans, often enough, came north with a chip on their shoulders. Memories of the Civil War were too fresh to be forgotten. The farmers who barred passage to the herds, the Jayhawkers who robbed them, the townspeople who made money catering to their needs, the commission men who bought their cattle, the gamblers and saloon keepers who preyed upon them, even the marshals and law officers—almost all of these were Northerners. Each side regarded the other with hatred and suspicion. It did not take much to start a quarrel, or for the Texans, fierce in their pride, to feel that they were being taken advantage of, robbed, or cheated. As Teddy Blue explained it:

Most of them that came up with the trail herds, being from Texas and southerners to start with, was on the side of the South, and oh, but they were bitter. That was how a lot of them got killed, because they were filled full of the old dope about the war, and they wouldn't let an abolitionist arrest them. The marshals in these cow towns were usually northern men, and the Southerners wouldn't go back to Texas and hear people say: "He's a hell of a fellow. He let a Yankee lock him up." Down home one Texas Ranger could arrest the lot of them, but up North, you'd have to kill them first.

In 1870, the citizens of Abilene built a small stone jail on Texas Street across from the saloons. While it was being constructed the cowpunchers tore down the walls. After it was finished they shot off the lock from the door and freed the first prisoner, a black cook from a cow camp who had been locked up for disorderly conduct.

The town trustees decided that they needed their own marshal, but Abilene was a boisterous town and it was difficult to find men who would serve. The St. Louis police chief sent two officers to Abilene to take the job. But the cowboys heard of their coming and gave them

Bar-room brawl, an engraving
by Frederic Remington.

such a warm reception that the two officers returned to St. Louis that same evening.

The trustees then decided to hire Thomas J. Smith, a former New York policeman, who had been one of the first to apply for the job. T. C. Henry, then mayor of Abilene, tells how Smith had originally been turned down:

Smith had applied for the place a few days after the office of Town Marshal had been created, but while physically he was a giant in strength, his quiet ways, soft and low voice, and utter lack of anything like bravado had led the mayor to conclude that such a man could not be Marshal of Abilene.

After the incident with the St. Louis policemen the town trustees decided to give Smith a chance. He turned out to be one of the bravest and most unusual marshals in the history of the West. Henry, in his account, *Thomas James Smith of Abilene*, recalls the interview when Smith got the job, and what followed.

It was on a Saturday morning late in May, 1870, that Smith reappeared at my office. He said he believed he could handle the town.

"What plans do you propose to accomplish that?" I asked, anxious to get his ideas and to size him up. He replied that fire-arms must be given up; that whiskey and pistols were a combination beyond control.

I inquired if he really thought that he could enforce that ordinance.

"Yes," he said, "I think I can."

"When do you want to begin?" I asked.

"As well at once," he quietly replied.

Then I recited the oath of office to him as we stood there alone. Silently he moved off, and I watched him, with misgivings, disappear down town, a third of a mile away.

Almost immediately he encountered Big Hank, a cowboy desperado who had been loudest in boasts that no one would disarm him. He approached Smith and tauntingly asked him if he were the man who proposed to run the town. Smith said that he had been employed as Marshal, and that he would try to maintain order and enforce the law.

"What are you going to do about that gun ordinance?" asked Hank.

"See that it is obeyed," replied Smith; and then he quickly added, "I must trouble you to hand me yours."

With a coarse oath this was refused. Characteristically cool, Smith again made the demand, and again met with profanity and abuse. Instantly he sprang forward and landed a terrific blow which placed Big Hank hors de combat [out of action]. The Marshal took away the pistol, and ordered its owner at once to leave for camp, a command heeded with crest-fallen alacrity.

Despite all the knock-down, drag-out fights shown on television and in the movies, cowboys did not fight with their fists. They considered this beneath their dignity; cowpunchers needed their hands to do their work, and they could not afford to damage them. If they intended to fight, they fought with guns.

T. C. Henry, continuing his account of Smith, gives a rather typical western picture of a confrontation between the Marshal and a "bad man," Wyoming Frank, who boasted that he would give up his gun to no one. But it is an interesting incident because it led to the disarming of the town and taking guns away from everybody. Marshal Smith understood clearly enough the obvious truth that you cannot really have law and order when almost everybody has the right to carry a gun.

Smith came quietly down the middle of the street . . . and presently confronted the advancing bully. Frank began backing off as Smith advanced quietly, calling for his gun. Frank steadily retired, maneuvering for time and space in which to draw his pistol and thus have the drop on Smith. To his courteous but firm demand, Frank exploded an insulting oath and vile epithet. Quick as a flash, Smith vaulted and, with a terrific double blow, sent his antagonist prone to the floor, and with the unbelted pistol vigorously belaboured the brute. . . .

For an instant all stood dazed and speechless, whereupon the saloon proprietor stepped from behind the bar and said to Smith: "That was the nerviest act I ever saw. You did your duty and that coward got what he deserved. Here is my gun. I reckon I'll not need it as long as you are marshal of this town."

That was a signal. Everyone pushed forward proferring Smith pistols. He quietly thanked them, and said: "Hand your guns to the bartender to keep until you want to get out to camp." From that moment Tom Smith was master. . . . No guns thereafter were openly worn on the streets of Abilene while Smith was Marshal.

Tom Smith was killed five months later, not by a Texas cowboy, but by a local Abilene farmer whom he

*

After a shoot-out.

was trying to arrest on a murder charge. The whole town mourned his passing.

The next Marshal of Abilene was Wild Bill Hickok, the frontier scout and Indian fighter. He was the opposite of Smith in appearance, personality, and action. Wild Bill depended upon his double-action Army pistols and his reputation as a dead shot. He did not enforce the law against gun-carrying in town, and usually could be found in a saloon. There were shootings and killings during his regime, but the summer that Hickok was Marshal was Abilene's last year as a cow town. His contract was not renewed.

A cowboy's time in town was brief. Very soon he had to go back home to Texas. It was the custom for the ranch owner who employed him to pay the cowpuncher's railroad fare back to the ranch. The horses as well as the cattle were sold at the end of a drive.

To think of Abilene, or of any cow town, as just a place where cowboys fought, gambled, and whored is to adopt a superficial approach. These towns were important commercial centers. Abilene itself did more than three million dollars of business a year.

The Cowboy's Lament
(See Acknowledgments, page 191)

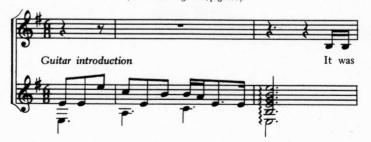

Guitar introduction   It was

ear - ly one morn - ing as I passed St. James Hos - pi - tal,

Lord, it was ear - ly one morn - ing, morn-ing month of

May, I looked in the win - dow and I spied a young

cow-boy, He was wrapped in white lin-en as cold as the clay.

It was early one morning as I passed St. James Hospital,
Lord, it was early one morning, morning month of May,
I looked in the window, and I spied a young cowboy,
He was wrapped in white linen as cold as the clay.

Says "Come mother, dear mother, and seat yourself nigh me,
And father, dear father, come sing me a song,
For my knee bones are achin' and my poor heart is breakin',
Well, I know I'm a poor cowboy, and I know I done wrong.

"It was once in the saddle I used to look handsome,
It was once in the saddle I used to go gay,
First took to drinking, and then took to gambling,
Got shot in the breast and I'm dying today.

"Get six young gamblers to carry my coffin,
Sixteen pretty whore gals to sing me a song
Tell them to bring 'long a bunch of them sweet-smelling roses,
So they won't smell me while they drive me along."

It was early one morning as I passed St. James Hospital,
Lord, one morning, morning month of May,
I looked in the window, and spied a young cowboy,
He was wrapped in white linen as cold as the clay.

THE EXTERMINATION OF
THE BUFFALO

With Abilene and other depots on the Kansas Pacific, a beginning had been made. The Texans had found railheads from which to ship their beef to northern buyers. The railway, at the same time that it was shipping cattle east, was moving immigrants west—small farmers anxious to settle the High Plains and bring them under the plow, to raise wheat rather than cattle.

In 1870, then, the Great Plains were on the edge of a gigantic transformation. But there was an obstacle to the systematic and total exploitation of this area by the white man. The Plains were the home of the buffalo and the Indian. Before the Longhorns and the steel plow could inherit the sod, the buffalo must be swept aside. If Indians raised a finger to prevent this, they too must be swept away and destroyed.

To say that the buffalo dominated the High Plains is no mere figure of speech. In the early 1800's their numbers were estimated at between sixty and seventy-five million; they provided the very foundation for Indian existence. George Catlin, the famous artist who roamed the West in the 1830's painting the Indians, pointed this out in his journal:

There are, by a fair calculation, more than 300,000 Indians who are now subsisting on the flesh of the buffaloes, and by these animals supplied with all the luxuries of life which they desire, as they know of none others. The great variety of uses to which they convert the body and other parts of that animal are almost incredible to the person who has not actually dealt among these people and closely studied their modes and customs. Every part of the flesh is converted into food, in one shape or another, and on it they entirely subsist. The robes of the animal are worn by the Indians instead of blankets; their skins when tanned are used as coverings for their lodges and for their beds; undressed [the skins] are used for constructing canoes, for saddles, for bridles, lariats, lassos and thongs. The horns are shaped into ladles and spoons . . . their bones are used for saddle trees, for war clubs, and scrapers for graining the robes, and others are broken up for the marrow-fat which is contained within them. Their sinews are used for strings and backs for their bows, for thread to string their beads and sew their dresses. The feet of the animal are boiled with their hoofs for the glue they contain, for fastening their arrow points, and many other uses. The hair from the head and shoulder, which is long, is twisted and braided into halters, and the tail is used for a fly brush.

Buffalo robes were a standard article of trade between the Indian peoples and the white men from the very first days of white settlement and exploration of the West.

King Beast of the Western Plains. Frequently weighing over 2,000 Pounds.

WESTERN ROBE AGENCY.

Picture of the buffalo, "King Beast of the
Western Plains," from the advertisement of a
trading firm.

Thick, shaggy, and warm, a good buffalo robe was a necessity for people traveling by horseback, sled, or carriage in the winter, and was much in demand in the East and in Europe. Buffalo fat also found a ready market, as it was used to make candles and soap.

The Indians, therefore, killed the buffalo freely, but did not reduce their numbers. The Indians, indeed, worshipped the bison herds, because they were the source of life and the basis of survival; in their hunting ceremonies they gave thanks to the gods for sending them the buffaloes whom they loved as brothers.

In the space of twelve brief years, from 1871 to 1883, the buffalo were swept from the prairies as though a plague had struck; from forty million their numbers were reduced to barely one hundred. In that instant of time, a great national heritage was wiped out, the wild life of the Plains was all but destroyed, and the culture and independent existence of the Plains Indians were obliterated.

How did this come about?

As soon as the white man appeared in the West he cursed it with the evils of his civilization. In the 1840's, emigrants bound for Oregon and Salt Lake City brought with them cholera and smallpox that took the lives of thousands of Plains Indians. In 1849 the gold seekers whitened the prairies with their wagons, killed the game, cut down scarce timber, devoured and burned off the grass, polluted the water holes and streams.

The Indians watched this invasion with alarm, but until the 1860's the damage was, relatively speaking, minor. Uncounted millions of buffalo still roamed the

Plains, and the herds were still so thick that travelers had to stop and wait for them to go by before they could continue. Wagon trains, cowboys with Longhorns, and even railroads had to pause in their travels. J. S. Campion, a young English traveler, wrote at that time:

The rolling prairies looked as though they might have been a tumultuous sea of monstrous waves, suddenly transmuted into solid ground, and covered with a brilliant carpet of green grass. It was an interminable repetition of lithe undulating hills. . . . And there, spread all over it, were the buffaloes; the nearest, within a mile; the farthest—who could tell how far away? The whole country was alive with them. They were there in troops, in squadrons, in divisions, in armies!

It was the building of the railroads across the Plains that gave the signal for the first really serious and intensive attack upon the buffalo and Indian prairie ecology. The survey parties, the track and construction crews, and the soldiers assigned to protect them all needed meat; the professional buffalo hunter made his first appearance.

One of the most famous of these men was William F. Cody, later to be known as Buffalo Bill. In his autobiography, Cody tells of his agreement with the railroad to provide buffalo meat for the crews:

The western end of the Kansas Pacific was at this time in the heart of the buffalo country. Twelve hundred men were employed in the construction of the road. The Indians were very troublesome and it was difficult to obtain

fresh meat for the hands. The company therefore con-
cluded to engage expert hunters to kill buffalo.

Having heard of my experience and success as a buffalo hunter, Goodard Brothers, who had the contract for
feeding the men, made me a good offer to become their
hunter. They said they would require about twelve buffaloes a day—twenty-four hams and twelve humps, as
only the humps and hind-quarters of each animal were
utilized. This work was dangerous. Indians were riding
all over the section . . . and my duties would require me
to journey from five to ten miles from the railroad every
day in order to secure the game, accompanied only by
one man with a light wagon to haul the meat back to
camp.

At the same time, the railroads encouraged hunting
the buffalo for sport. In this they continued a tradition
that had begun before the Civil War. In 1854, for example, an Irish nobleman, St. George Gore, organized
an elaborate expedition; he took along 40 servants, 112
horses, 3 cows, and 27 wagons to carry his guns, bed-
stead, wines, and library. Gore's hunt lasted, on and off,
about three years, and cost about half a million dollars.
In one winter alone he killed more than 2,000 buffalo,
1,600 deer and elk, 105 bears, and various other animals.

By 1868, catering to the tastes of both European and
American sportsmen, the railroads were running excursion trains into the buffalo country. These trains were
shooting galleries on wheels from which the "sportsmen"
could kill easily with no danger or inconvenience to
themselves. A typical placard posted at the Lawrence,
Kansas, station of the Kansas Pacific read:

RAILWAY EXCURSION AND BUFFALO HUNT

An excursion train will leave Leavenworth at 8 A.M. and Lawrence at 10 A.M. for

Sheridan

on Tuesday, October 27, 1868, and return on Friday. This train will stop at the principal stations both going and coming. Ample time will be had for a grand buffalo

HUNT ON THE PLAINS

Buffalo are so numerous along the road that they are shot from the cars nearly every day. On our last excursion our party killed twenty buffaloes in a hunt of six hours.

All passengers can have refreshments at reasonable prices.

Tickets for round trip from Leavenworth: $10.00.

Until 1870 buffalo hides had been considered worthless. But in 1871–1872 two Pennsylvania tanners were successful in developing a process that turned the hides into usable leather. Stronger and more elastic than steer hide, buffalo leather could now be used for industrial belting in factories, and for leather furniture and for floor and wall covering. It could also be used in the manufacture of carriages, sleighs, and hearses.

Thus the demand for hides grew by leaps and bounds during the 1870's, and turned into an avalanche. Previously the buffalo had been killed for its meat, for robes, and for amusement. This was as nothing to the slaughter that now got under way. Colonel Richard Dodge, com-

manding officer of Fort Dodge, and a keen observer of
life in the West, tells what happened next:

By wagon, on horseback and a-foot, the pot-hunters
poured in, and soon the unfortunate buffalo was without
a moment's peace or rest. Though hundreds of thou-
sands of skins were sent to market, they scarcely indi-
cated the slaughter that from want of skill in shooting,
and want of knowledge in preserving the hides of those
slain, on the part of these green hunters, one hide sent
to market represented three, four, or even five dead buf-
falo.

The merchants in the small towns along the railroads
were not slow to take advantage of this new opening.
They furnished outfits, arms, ammunition, etc. to needy
parties, and established great trades, by which many now
ride in their carriages.

The buffalo melted away like snow before a summer's
sun. Congress talked of interfering, but only talked.
Winter and summer, in season and out of season, the
slaughter went on.

As buffalo grew scarce in Kansas, hunters started crossing the Arkansas river and pursuing the buffalo south of
it. Hunters became more efficient, learning to kill as
effortlessly and quickly as possible. John R. Cook, himself a buffalo hunter, described what the hunters did.

It happened about midday. There must have been
more than a thousand of them. After drinking they came
out on a flat about 150 yards from the creek. There they
stopped and commenced laying down. I was not more
than 80 steps away when I began shooting. I shot a

tremendously large bull first. All he did was to "cringe" a little. Not half those lying down rose at the sound of the gun. . . . After I had killed twenty-five that I knew of, the smoke from the gun commenced to hang low, and was slow in disappearing.

Cook noticed that even while the shooting was going on, the buffaloes would lie down quietly, "apparently unconcerned about the destruction going on about them." They had never acquired, evidently, as other animals had, an instinctive fear of man. As the herd finally started to move off, Cook counted his kill; there were eighty-eight in all, "their eyes glassy in death." His colleague Charlie commented that "this is the prettiest sight I ever beheld."

As soon as the hunters had finished their killing, the skinners began their job. It was hard, dirty, smelly, and backbreaking work. Hordes of flies swarmed around. Working in pairs, the skinners rolled the dead animal upon his back and slit his hide along the belly from neck to tail. Then they literally peeled the skin off, leaving the carcass for wolves, coyotes, and buzzards. Experienced skinners working together in this way were able to skin as many as fifty buffalo a day.

The Buffalo Skinners
(See Acknowledgments, page 191)

Come all you jolly cowboys and listen to my song,
There are not many verses, it will not detain you long;
It's concerning some young fellows who did agree to go
And spend one summer pleasantly on the range of the buffalo.

It happened in Jacksboro in the spring of seventy-three,
A man by the name of Crego came stepping up to me,
Saying, "How do you do, young fellow, and how would you
    like to go
And spend one summer pleasantly on the range of the buf-
    falo?"

"It's me being out of employment," this to Crego I did say,
"This going out on the buffalo range depends upon the pay.
But if you will pay good wages and transportation too,
I think, sir, I will go with you to the range of the buffalo."

It's now we've crossed Pease River, our troubles have begun.
The first damned tail I went to rip, Christ! how I cut my
    thumb!
While skinning the damned old stinkers our lives wasn't a
    show,
For the Indians watched to pick us off while skinning the
    buffalo.

Our meat was buffalo rump and iron wedge bread,
And all we had to sleep on was a buffalo robe for a bed;
The fleas and graybacks worked on us, oh boys, it was not
    slow,
I'll tell you there's no worse hell on earth than the range of
    the buffalo.

The season being near over, old Crego he did say
The crowd had been extravagant, was in debt to him that
    day.
We coaxed him and begged him, and still it was no go—
We left his damned old bones to bleach on the range of the
    buffalo.

Oh, it's now we've crossed Pease River and homeward we are
    bound,
No more in that hell-fired country shall we ever be found.

Go home to our wives and sweethearts, tell others not to go,
For God's forsaken the buffalo range and the damned old
   buffalo.

By 1873 buffalo were scarce on both sides of the Arkansas River. Cook, who had been impressed by the wild
beauty of the country as well as by the teeming abundance of its wildlife, began to have second thoughts
about the mindless slaughter:

> At times I asked myself, "What would you do, John
> R. Cook, if you had been a child of this wonderfully
> prolific game region, your ancestors back through count-
> less ages, according to traditional history, having roamed
> the vast solitudes as free as the air they breathed? What
> would you do if some outside interloper should come
> in and start a ruthless slaughter upon the very soil you
> had grown from childhood upon, and that you believed
> you alone had all the rights by occupancy that could
> possibly be given one? Yes, what would you do?"

Cook, if he had been a native son of the Plains, would
have done, no doubt, exactly what the Indian peoples
did. From the first moment that the white man came to
pollute, slaughter, and destroy their land, they fought
back as best they could. On the one side there were raids
and massacres of the white settlers; on the other, a policy
of cold-blooded revenge and extermination that spared
neither men, women nor children, and that reached its
climax in 1890, when the U.S. Army murdered the Sioux
chief Sitting Bull and approximately two hundred of his
people.
   Indian resistance merely underlined the determination

of the Federal Government and the army to allow the killing of the buffalo to go on unchecked, for the authorities saw in the destruction of the buffalo the surest way to end the Indian wars and to break the power of the Plains tribes. General Phil Sheridan testified as follows before the Texas Legislature, when they were considering a bill to protect the buffalo:

Instead of stopping the hunters you ought to give them a hearty vote of thanks, and give each hunter a medal of bronze with a dead buffalo on one side and a discouraged Indian on the other. These men have done more in the last two years, and will do more in the next year, to settle the vexed Indian question than the regular army has done in the last thirty. They are destroying the Indians' commissary, and it is a well known fact that an army losing its base of supplies is at a great disadvantage. Send the hunters powder and lead if you will, but for the sake of peace let them kill, skin, and sell until the buffalo are exterminated. Then your prairies can be covered with cattle and the cowboy, who follows the hunter as a second forerunner of an advanced civilization.

In the winter of 1876–1877 the killing reached its height. 1500 hunters and skinners were kept busy in the Texas Panhandle. Everywhere was the booming of the guns as the buffalo faced a hail of lead.

By 1878–1879 buffalo were hard to find; commercial hide-hunting was drawing to a close in Texas. Some hunters turned to other occupations; others went in search of the herds that still roamed the northern plains in Montana, Wyoming, and the Dakotas. There, again, the familiar story of slaughter was repeated.

Curing buffalo hides, an illustration from
Harper's Weekly, 1874.

By the fall of 1883, of the sixty to seventy-five million buffalo that had once roamed the plains, only a few scattered surviviors, numbering two or three hundred, remained. The bones, picked clean by wolves and buzzards, whitened the prairies from Texas to the Canadian border.

They did not lie there long, for they were a source of revenue for the railroads; shipped east and ground into meal they could be used as agricultural fertilizer. Robert Wright, one of the early settlers of Dodge City, recalled:

One of Dodge City's great industries was the bone trade. It certainly was immense. There were great stacks of bones piled up by the railroad tracks, hundreds of tons of them. It was a sight to see them. They were stacked up way above the tops of the box cars, and often there were insufficient cars to move them.

The bones were a godsend to the early settlers, for they were [the settler's] main stock in trade for a long, long time; and if it had not been for the bone industry, many poor families would have suffered for the very necessaries of life. Many poor emigrants and settlers came to Kansas with nothing but an old wagon and a worn span of horses, a large family of helpless children, and a few dogs— nothing else. No money, no work of any kind to be had, when by gathering buffalo bones they could make a living and get a start. Game was all killed off, and starvation staring them in the face; bones were their only salvation, and this industry saved them. They gathered and piled them up in large piles during the winter, and hauled them to Dodge at times when they had nothing else to do.

THE BONANZA YEARS

The buffalo were exterminated; the power of the Plains people was broken and the survivors herded onto reservations. The Great Plains lay open to the cattlemen. Like an endless river the cattle began to stream northwards and westwards into Montana, Wyoming, and the Dakotas, and to inherit the entire kingdom of the grasslands. The stockmen had made the discovery that the Texas Longhorns could survive the cold of the northern winters, and that they could grow fat by grazing on the rich northwestern grasses.

As the cattle moved north, Texas horses and Texas cowboys went with them. Many of the cowpunchers stayed up north to work as ranch hands the year round because the pay and food were usually better than back home. Settlers in the Dakotas and Montana grumbled that "a man couldn't step outside his cabin and spit without hitting a Texas cowboy!"

Thus in the early 1880's the cattle business entered its boom period. The bad times that had plagued the economy during the 70's were over, and the demand for meat was larger than ever. America had become a beef-eating nation, and there was a growing demand for

American meat in Europe. By the end of 1881, 110,000,-
000 pounds of frozen beef were being shipped to Great
Britain alone. The invention of canning machinery and
the marketing of canned beef further increased demand
and drove up prices.

To invest in cattle and to grow rich from raising and
selling them now became a speculative mania that
gripped American business leadership and people with
money to invest in both the United States and Europe.
This mania was just one expression of the period in
American history that is known by a label Mark Twain
gave it, "The Gilded Age." At that time vast fortunes
were being amassed by tycoons like John D. Rockefeller,
J. P. Morgan, Andrew Carnegie, Cornelius Vanderbilt,
and Philip Armour. These men justified their great
wealth as a reward for their industry, organizing ability,
and high intelligence. Wealthy men, wrote Andrew
Carnegie, had it in their power to be, and ought to be,
the greatest benefactors of society.

This theme, *get rich*, was preached in the newspapers
and also from the pulpits of America. Reverend Russell
H. Conwell, for example, one of the most articulate
spokesmen for the philosophy of the Gilded Age, delivered his famous lecture, *Acres of Diamonds*, 6,000
times in forty years. For two hours each time he held
audiences fascinated with his message:

*I say you ought to be rich; you have no right to be
poor. To live and not to be rich is a misfortune, and it
is doubly a misfortune, because you could have been rich
just as well as be poor. You and I know that there are
some things more valuable than money, of course we*

Hays, Kansas, a Western cattle town, 1885.

do. . . . Nevertheless the man of common sense also knows that there is not one of those things that is not greatly enhanced by the use of money. Money is power. Love is the grandest thing on God's earth, but fortunate is the lover who has plenty of money. For a man to say "I do not want money," is to say, "I do not wish to do any good to my fellow men."

In actual fact, the men who made money out of the cattle or oil or steel business lavished it not upon love but upon luxury. William Henry Vanderbilt, grandson of Cornelius Vanderbilt the steamboat king, spent $100,-000 to move Cleopatra's Needle from Egypt to Central Park. He built two great townhouses on 52nd Street for his daughters and himself; in the process he spent $3,-000,000 and employed 600 workmen for a year and a half. Then, on March 26, 1883, Vanderbilt and his wife had a fine housewarming.

Supper was served in the gymnasium, which had been transformed into a tropical garden with orchids, bougan-villea, and palm trees. The guests came in fancy dress that had taken months to get ready. Cornelius Vander-bilt appeared as Louis XIV of France, the Sun King, and his wife as the Queen of Electric Light.

Now in the 1880's, the smell of money was in the cattle business. The gold-diggers and wealth-getters flocked to it like moths to a candle. A delirium swept the East as men begged and borrowed money to put it into cattle and ranches. Typical of this spirit was a letter written by a Connecticut judge who was raising capital to form a corporation that would breed cattle. "The profits," wrote Judge Sherwood, are enormous. There is no business like it in the world, and the whole secret of it is, it costs nothing to feed the cattle. They grow without eating your money. They literally raise themselves.

The cupidity of investors was also stimulated by the writings of professional promoters. One such book, *The Beef Bonanza, or How to Get Rich on the Plains,* was written by James Brisbin, lawyer and ex-army major. His work sold well in the East and phenomenally well in Great Britain. Brisbin cited examples of people who had struck it rich in the cattle business:

Mr. R. C. Keith of the North Platte, Nebraska, began raising cows in the fall of 1867 with 5 American cows. Each year he and his partner bought more cows. The total cost of the cattle from 1867 to 1873 inclusive, was under $50,000. This did not include expenses of ranch, herding, etc. . . . which, however, were small, as they had no land or timber to buy. They had several employees; their men cost $5.00 per month plus board. . . . They have sold and butchered cattle which brought them $12,000 profit. They have, remaining on hand, cattle worth $93,000. Thus they have made an enormous profit.

Brisbin urged people with surplus funds to invest in cattle rather than some other business. "Money invested in cattle," he wrote,

would realize a far larger profit . . . than if put into mining, lumber, iron, manufacturing, or land companies. Nothing, I believe, would beat associated capital in the cattle trade, unless it would be banking, and stockraising would probably fully compete with even banking as a means of profit on capital invested in large sums.

The cattle boom became the main topic of conversation in many an Eastern mansion and English drawing-room. Conservative gentlemen, who didn't know a beef steer from a milch cow, met in their clubs to discuss the beef bonanza over a glass of port. Aristocratic British families packed their offbeat and troublesome sons off to the West to engage in ranching and to sow their wild oats. Many thousands of acres in Wyoming, indeed, were bought up and taken over by British cattle companies. The Powder River Cattle Company, for example, included the Duke of Manchester and Lord Henry Neville among its directors. The King Ranch in San Antonio was the largest in the country and the property of a British syndicate.

Some investors were the victims of swindlers, but many ranches flourished and paid good dividends. The age of the so-called "cattle kings," or large-scale operations and absentee ownership, had arrived.

Cheyenne, Wyoming, became the social center of the northwestern cattle empire, and the luxurious Cheyenne Club was the headquarters of the wealthy cattlemen and managers. It was one of the first clubs in the United States to substitute electric lights for gas lamps. In the summer, cattlemen sat on its wide porch sipping cool drinks and reading the *London Times*. Tennis, baseball, and dancing were the preferred amusements. The club served imported wines, chilled champagne, and fresh oysters; members put on dinner jackets for the evening meal.

The Cheyenne Club.

John Clay, a Scotsman and manager of several large western ranches, has told about the Cheyenne Club in his book *My Life on the Range*:

It was a cosmopolitan place. Under its roof reticent Britisher, cautious Scot, exuberant Irishman, careful Yankee, confident Bostonian, worldly New Yorker, chivalrous Southerner, and delightful Canadian, all found a welcome home . . . a motley group full of ginger and snap, with more energy than business sense.

There at the club they met and they fashioned it after eastern and foreign methods. The foreigner was caught up by the ease and luxury of its café and dining room. There was an atmosphere of success among its members. They spent money freely, for all along the line there was a swelling song of victory.

The Cheyenne Club was a symbol of the changes taking place in the cattle industry. Owners invested their money but not their time or themselves. Absentee ownership and big corporations were becoming dominant, setting aside the old intimate relationship of a cattleman with his cowpunchers. The cowboy did not have the same feelings of loyalty to the outfit as he had had when ranches were smaller and owners worked side by side with their men. An economic and social gulf grew up between the hands and the employers. Cowboys called their white-shirted, black-coated employers "herefords" after the white-and-black cattle of that breed. Foreigners they referred to as "elegants" and "velvet britchers."

The cowboy was still a working man working for the same small wages; he felt left out of the growing prosperity. In March, 1883, down in the Texas Panhandle

The Becker sisters branding cattle on their Colorado ranch.

town of Tascosa, there took place the first cowboy strike noted in our history. Fifty cowboys employed by the LX, LIT, and LS ranches, all large outfits, handed their bosses a written notice:

We, the undersigned cowboys of Canadian River, do by these presents agree to bind ourselves into the following obligations, viz.: First, that we will not work for less than $50 per month, and we furthermore agree no one shall work for less than $50 per month after the 31st of March.

Second, good cooks shall also receive $50 per month.

Third, anyone running an outfit shall not work for less than $75 per month. Anyone violating the above obligations shall suffer the consequences.

Current wages were $25 a month. The LIT offered $35, but the cowboys held firm.

News of the strike spread rapidly all over the range land and generated much sympathy. *The Caldwell Commercial* printed this comment on March 29:

The strike of the cowboys in the Panhandle seems to be more serious than was first thought. The boys threaten to prevent [other] men taking their place. It is thought a compromise will be effected. Cowboys have some knowledge of the immense profits cattle owners are making, and it should not be at all surprising if they asked fair wages for what is the hardest kind of work.

The strike was unsuccessful; many men were drifting into the county looking for work and the ranchers had no difficulty hiring some of them to work in the spring roundup. After about a month, their funds exhausted, the strikers were forced to return to their jobs at the old pay.

In March, 1886, in Colfax County, New Mexico, eighty cowboys and small ranchers met to form an association called Northern New Mexico Small Cattlemen and Cowboys' Union. They issued a statement of purpose:

No cattle owners who employ more than two men are to be received into the union.

We, the cowboys, pledge ourselves to look after the interests of small cattlemen, who are members, and the small cattlemen pledge themselves to do all in their power for the interest of the cowboys.

But the union never really got going. It fell a victim to the blizzards of 1886 and 1887 that completely changed the life of the open range, and, along with the collapse of the cattle boom, put an end to the lush years of the 1880's.

Goodbye Old Paint

Good
bye, old paint, I'm a leav - in' Chey - enne, Good
bye, old paint, I'm a leav - in' Chey - enne. I'm
leav - in' Chey - enne, I'm off to Mon - tan, Good

bye, old paint, I'm a leav - in' Chey - enne.

Goodbye, old Paint, I'm a-leavin' Cheyenne,
Goodbye, old Paint, I'm a-leavin' Cheyenne.
I'm ridin' old Paint, I'm leadin' old Dan,
Goodbye, old Paint, I'm a-leavin' Cheyenne.

Goodbye, old Paint, I'm a-leavin' Cheyenne,
Goodbye, old Paint, I'm a-leavin' Cheyenne.
I'm off to Montan' to throw the houlihan,
Goodbye, old Paint, I'm a-leavin' Cheyenne.

Goodbye, old Paint, I'm a-leavin' Cheyenne,
Goodbye, old Paint, I'm a-leavin' Cheyenne.
They feed in the coulees, they water in the draw,
Goodbye, old Paint, I'm a-leavin' Cheyenne.

CATASTROPHE: THE BLIZZARDS
OF 1886 AND 1887

The autumn of 1885 was a warm, soft, and pleasant one
—perfect Indian summer weather. The cattle grazed on
the open plains and grew fat. Since the blizzards of 1879
and 1881, the winters had been mild.

Though market prices were low, cattlemen, in general,
were optimistic. Prices were bound to go up again. It
would be a good winter, and in the spring sales would be
brisk and the bonanza would continue. Ranchers relaxed
for the winter with peaceful minds and thoughts of
golden profits.

The last day of the year dawned mild and clear, but
by noon a cold drizzle began and the temperature started
to drop. The rain turned to a fine, white, powdery snow
swept along by violent winds. The snow clung to every
weed, bush, and tree. Blown along by an insane, howling
wind, it blinded cattle, men, and horses. The whole eastern portion of the range country, from the Dakotas to
Texas, was in the grip of the worst blizzard in the history
of the West.

The storm lasted three days and three nights. The first
night, eighteen inches of snow fell and the temperature

plunged to 20° below zero. No trains or mail deliveries were able to get through. The snow continued and temperatures stayed below zero for weeks.

An anonymous cattleman, writing in *Prose and Poetry of the Live Stock Industry*, described the storm:

The sun was hidden behind a leaden sheet of cloud that dipped below the entire circle of the horizon but was thicker and darker in the north and northwest. There was a strange feeling in the quiet, colder-growing air. The silence of the range became deeper and more oppressive. The cattle stop feeding, raise their heads and look uneasily toward the north.

They do not return to the grass, but presently begin to move restlessly. The air is colder and is in motion, and with its movement there is a quivering and a moaning rustle is heard in the sagebrush and the swaying grass. The cattle shake their heads, and as they run here and there they mutter, and the sounds of loud bellowing comes from them. Their understanding of Nature's ways is better than that of man.

Then, with a sweeping rush, the blizzard itself whirls down upon them. Horizon, hills, draws, and all the rest vanish from sight in an instant in the whirl and swirl of sleet and fine snow that sting and smart all living flesh they strike.

The cattle turn their heads from the blast and huddle close like a flock of sheep. Bleating calves that were left outside try to find shelter by pushing themselves into the huddle or crawling under the bodies of beasts on their flanks. The close-packed mass now is blanketed with snow and sleet. Presently some steers at the head, where they had been shielded a little, unsteadily move forward. Those next behind follow in a faltering way, and soon the entire herd is in motion. The cattle are drifting with the cruel storm, and where and how the drift will end no one knows.

As the cattle moved onward in the fury of the storm, they were guided only by the course of the freezing gale. Icicles formed and hung down over their eyes, blinding their sight. The herd soon was strung out in a line like that of a trail-herd. The stronger and better conditioned were at the head, while back in the "drag" the weaklings were beginning to fall down and out. Some became detached from the column and staggered on alone—but not far.

The driving wind swept the snow into the ravines and filled them from side to side. When the groping cattle came to the verge of one of these pitfalls, the way across appeared to be a level continuation of the ground-surface on which they trod. On they went, and were plunged into the death-trap, tumbling upon each other in a sickening heap of struggling, bellowing half-frozen, crippled, smothering beasts. The relentless storm swept more snow in upon them and covered them over.

Sometimes a bunch of blizzard-driven cattle would seek refuge under the lee of a bluff, where they kept the snow trampled down upon the ground they occupied. But it piled up around them higher and higher and walled them in. The grass under their feet soon was eaten out by the roots, and as they could not escape from the trap, the poor creatures slowly starved to death.

The heat of the cattle's bodies melted some of the sleet and snow with which they were pelted, and the water, trickling on the hair, became ice again, within a quarter of an inch of the animal's hides. Small masses of accumulated ice locked the jaws of many of them. Icicles formed on the points of their bodies, and as they became larger and heavier and were made to swing by the movements of the cattle to which they were attached, they began to pull the hair out by the roots. This was continued until the icicle was released, leaving a patch of bare, red skin.

So this tragedy of the cattle-range went on to its end. The trail of the drifting herd was marked here and there in every mile by the bodies of its members that had reached the limit of their endurance and had fallen in their tracks and died.

Neither man nor beast could live in that terrible cold and wind. Cowboys, more brave than wise, tried to stay with their herds and turn them to safety before the storm. A former rancher and western writer, Emerson Hough, in his book, *Story of the Cowboy*, eloquently told the fate of two such cowpunchers.

In a few moments the whole herd is covered with a blanket of white. The two men who are now up with the herd strive to break apart this blanket of white, riding along the edges with bent heads, seeking to open out the cattle so that they can get them moving. It is useless; the white veil shuts down too sternly. The men can no longer breathe. Their eyes are blinded by the stinging rifts of fine ice. They are separated in the storm. A shout is answered by a shout, but though they ride one toward the other as best they may one can not find him now, forever the voice calling seems to shift and evade as

An artist's impression of the blizzard, Harper's
Weekly, February 27, 1886.

though the spirits used it mockingly. Crack! Crack! comes the note of a six-shooter, but how small, how far away it is! Again and again, and again also the answer! These two men have not lost their heart. They will yet find each other. They will turn the herd, they two alone, here on the wide, white plain, in this mystery of moving white. But where was the last shot? It sounded half a mile away. It might have been a hundred yards.

There comes a mightier wail of the wind, a more vindictive rush of the powdery snow. All trace of the landscape is now absolutely gone. The cowboy has wheeled his horse, but he knows not which way he heads. The hills may be this way or that. A strange, numb, confusing mental condition comes to him. He crouches down in the saddle, his head dropping, as he raises his arm yet again, and fires another shot, almost his last. He dreams he hears an answer, and he calls again hoarsely. The scream of the wind and the rumbling of the voices of the cattle drown out all other sounds. He is in with the herd. His partner is in with it too. But neither he nor they both will ever turn or direct this herd. This he knows with sinking heart. They are lost, all lost together, out here upon the pitiless plains.

More than a hundred persons died in Kansas alone, and over three hundred in the whole West, many of them cowboys. Settlers were trapped in their thin wooden huts, and froze to death.

In the Texas Panhandle, Les Cator, a rancher looking for his cattle, came upon a nester's wagon. The dead horses were still in harness. Cator looked inside the wagon tarp, and his heart sank. There he saw huddled together and frozen to death a father, mother, and three small children.

On the Kansas prairies, a father returned from town to his homestead. He found the walls blown down and scattered, the seven members of his family frozen in the snow.

Many ranchers lost between fifty and eighty-five per cent of their stock. The Reynolds brothers lost every one of their seven thousand steers. Before the storm the Circle M ranch had had six thousand cattle; in the spring they rounded up one hundred and fifty survivors.

A Kansas rancher was offered $25,000 for his herd a few days before the storm. Afterward he sold the balance for $500. Texas Red Cochran had driven his herd of 2,300 steers up to South Dakota to fatten on the range during the winter. When spring came he was left with fifty head of cattle. Ruined and heavily in debt, Red was forced back to being a working cowboy rather than a rancher. In similar fashion hundreds of outfits, both large and small, were wiped out.

The spring of 1886 found the Plains covered with dead and bloated cattle. The perfume of the Plains flowers was lost in the stink of death. The only profit came to the skinners who took the hides and later gathered the bones. Wolves, coyotes, and buzzards, too, grew fat that spring.

The cattlemen, in their greed for profits, had overstocked the range and neglected to take adequate steps for the protection of their cattle in the hard Plains winter. They paid the penalty in financial ruin. But there were also other penalties that the nation as a whole would pay for this folly. Lincoln Lang, a rancher in the Dakotas, noted that

everywhere now, were to be found filthy trampled mud holes where once had been clear running springs . . . where the wild-fowl had luxuriated but a little while before. Rank and even poisonous weed growths, heretofore unknown, were becoming increasingly in evidence all over the country. The glorious buttes were becoming more and more scarred and defoliated. The wonderful wild plum . . . for some more or less obscure reason— possibly overfertilization of the bushes by livestock seeking shelter among them—was ceasing to bear. Many varieties of migratory birds were seen no more. Game was rapidly growing scarce. . . .

Wyoming, Colorado, Montana, and the western Dakotas had escaped the blizzard of 1886. But their turn was now to come.

Throughout the range lands, the summer of 1886 was unusually dry. A hot wind shrivelled the grasses and dried up the streams and rivers. Lang noted that

like a huge, sullen, glowing ball, the sun arose each morning through a cloud of haze that seemed to have settled upon the country. . . . Temperature ranging up to 120° in the shade was common.

As the season progressed there was a continuous succession of prairie fires and a continuous battle of cowboys and rangehands to stamp them out.

A haze of smoke hung over the prairies from the great fires. Dust, ashes, and cinders floated through the air, covered the range, drifted into the ranch houses. *The Rocky Mountain Husbandman* reported in August:

There has hardly been an evening in the last week that the red glare of the fire demon has not lit up out mountain ridges, while our exchanges bring news of disastrous fires in all parts of the Territory.

The drought had also spread into the Midwestern corn belt and created a shortage of feed. Chicago beef prices had been falling steadily. There was no demand for cattle. The bottom seemed to have dropped out of the industry. The cattle that would have been sold that summer were held back by the cattlemen and left out on the already overcrowded range. The cattle that survived the summer were in poor condition when autumn started, thin and weak, with little resistance to cold weather.

The winter of 1886–1887 was heralded as a bad one. All signs pointed to it. Hermann Hagedorn, another rancher and a neighbor of Roosevelt in the Dakotas, described the omens in his book, *Roosevelt in the Badlands*:

Nature was busier than she had ever been in the memory of the oldest hunters in that region in "fixin' up her folks for hard times." The muskrats along the creeks were building their houses to twice their customary height; the walls were thicker than usual and the muskrats' fur was longer and heavier than any old-timer had ever known it to be. The beavers were working by day as well as by night cutting the willow brush, and observant eyes noted that they were storing twice their usual winter's supply. The birds were acting strangely. The ducks and geese, which ordinarily flew south in October, that autumn had a month earlier already departed. The snowbirds and the cedar birds were bunched in the thickets fluttering around by the thousands in the cane breaks, obviously restless and uneasy. The Arctic owls, who came only in hard winters, were about.

The cattle and horses were growing unusually long coats. Snow began to fall in October; late in December the weather turned very cold, registering 34° to 44° below zero until mid-February. Early in January, 1887, came the worst blizzard of many winters past—sixteen inches of snow fell in sixteen hours. Hagedorn described the experience in the Dakotas:

The snow was like the finest powder, driving through every crack and nail hole, and piling snowdrifts within the houses as well as without.

"Upon getting up in the morning," said Lincoln Lang long afterward, describing the storm, "the house was intensely cold, with everything that could freeze, frozen solid. As we opened our front door, we were confronted with a solid wall of snow reaching to the eaves of the house. There was no drift over the back door, looking north, but, as I opened it, I was blown almost from my feet by the swirl of the snow, which literally filled the air, so that it was impossible to see any of the surrounding ranch-buildings or even the fence, less than 50 feet distant. It was like a tornado of pure white dust or very fine sand, icy cold, and stinging like a whip lash."

Blizzard followed blizzard. For the men and women on the scattered ranches, it was a period of intense strain and privation; but for the cattle, wandering over the wind-swept world of snow and ice, these terrible months brought an affliction without parallel.

Late in January came a warm southern wind that partly melted the snow. But this was followed at once by another cold blast that turned the ground into solid ice. Teddy Blue, who was working as a cowboy in Montana that year, described the cowpunchers' struggles to save cattle now tormented with hunger and thirst:

The cattle drifted down on all the rivers, and untold thousands went down the air holes. On the Missouri we lost I don't know how many that way. They would walk out on the ice and the ones behind would push the front ones in. The cowpunchers worked like slaves to move them back in the hills, but as all the outfits cut their forces down every winter, they were shorthanded. No one knows how they worked but themselves. They saved thousands of cattle. Think of riding all day in a blinding snow storm, the temperature fifty and sixty below zero, and no dinner. You'd get one bunch of cattle up the hill and another one would be coming down behind you, and it was all so slow, plunging after them through the deep snow that way! You'd have to fight every step of the road. The horses' feet were cut and bleeding from the heavy crust, and the cattle had the hair and hide worn off their legs to the knees and hooks. It was surely hell to see big four-year-old steers just able to stagger along. It was the same all over Wyoming, Montana and Colorado, western Nebraska and western Kansas.

All through the range country, cowboys did their best to help the stricken cattle. In *Montana: High, Wide,*

From Once a Week magazine, November 26,
1889.

and Handsome, Joseph Kinsey Howard paints a picture of their heroism:

Cowboys donned two suits of heavy underwear, two pairs of wool socks, wool pants, two woolen shirts, overalls, leather chaps, wool gloves under leather mittens, blanket-lined overcoats and fur caps. Before putting on their socks they walked in the snow in their bare feet, then rubbed them dry vigorously. After pulling on their riding boots they stood in water, then outdoors until an airtight sheath of ice had formed on the boots. Sometimes instead of the riding boots they wore moccasins and overshoes or sheepskin-lined "packs."

Thus prepared, they mounted and fought their way through the snow to extricate cattle stuck in drifts, tried to herd dying beasts into the sheltered ravines and head them off from treacherous rivers. They blackened their faces and eye sockets with lamp-black or burnt matches to forestall snow blindness, or they cut holes in their black neckerchiefs and masked their faces, bandit-fashion. They strained and gasped as the icy air stabbed into their lungs and stomachs; they froze hands and feet and many of them died. Their bodies, frozen stiff, were lashed on the backs of their horses and borne back to the ranch houses, to be thrust into snowbanks until a chinook came, because the ground could not be broken for graves.

For all this they got no medals, nor expected any. A cowboy's job was to look after the herd; he was being paid for it—$40 a month. But hundreds of ranchers and riders underwent such hardships in that dreadful winter that they forsook the range forever, crippled in body and spirit.

As for the sufferings of the Indian peoples in their scattered reservations and camps, no pen has recorded them. A dispatch from Fort Keogh in the Dakotas to the *New York World*, February 14, 1887, observed that

The Indians seem to have caught it harder than any other human creatures in the country. . . . A number of Nez Perce Indians, a remnant of Chief Joseph's famous band, who fought General Miles and Howard so stubbornly, have been snowed in on Colville Reservation. Four feet of "beautiful snow" prevented hunting parties and many died from cold and hunger. During the latter part of January fifty lodges of Crow Indians camped on Clark's Fork came near dying. Many did perish, but the majority managed to sustain life by eating the cattle that died in the snow-drifts.

The Nez Perces, referred to here, were a mountain people from Idaho, who often hunted on the Plains. Under Chief Joseph they had conducted in 1877 the most famous of patriot struggles against white invasion. Rather than have their hunting lands stolen from them they took to the war path, were defeated after a brave and brilliant resistance, and sent into exile in Oklahoma. The Colville reservation, to which many of the braves were finally sent, was in the state of Washington.

Early in March, 1887, the snows began to melt, and the horror of the winter was over. Ice-encrusted cattle had staggered into towns and ranches, bawling pitifully. They had knocked down gates, huddled against buildings, pushed in doors, smashed windows in their efforts to find warmth and protection. They had eaten the tar paper off the sides of shacks, devoured the branches, roots, and bark of trees. Exhausted, shrunken, and starving, they had perished.

The spring thaw revealed the extent of the tragedy.

We suddenly heard a roar above that of the running water, coming from the direction of the Little Missouri, and hurrying there saw a sight, once seen, never to be forgotten. The river was out of its banks clear up to the cottonwoods, and out on to the bottom, going down in a raging, muddy torrent, literally full of huge, grinding ice-cakes, up-ending and rolling over each other as they went, tearing each other and everything in their course in the effort to get out and away. The spectacle held us spellbound. None of us had ever seen anything to compare with it, for the spring freshets of other years had been mild affairs compared to this. But there was something else that had never been seen before, and doubtless will never be seen again, for as we gazed we could see countless carcasses of cattle going down with the ice, rolling over and over as they went, so that at times all four of the stiffened legs of a carcass would point skyward as it turned under the impulsion of the swiftly moving current and the grinding ice-floes. Continuously carcasses seemed to be going down while others kept bobbing up at one point or another to replace them.

And this terrible drama continued, not for an hour or for a few hours, but for days. With them went our hopes. One had only to stand by the river bank a few minutes and watch the grim procession ceaselessly going down, to realize in full the depth of the tragedy that had been enacted within the past few months.

Between a million and a million and a half head of cattle, sheep, horses, and mules had died. Ranchers in Montana, Wyoming, Colorado, and the Dakotas were wiped out as badly as the more easterly ranchers had been the past year. Teddy Blue tells what the cowboys found in the spring.

The coulees in some places were piled deep with cattle where they had sought shelter and died, and the ones that were left were nothing but skin and bone and so weak they could scarcely stand. That was the story behind Charlie Russell's picture, "The Last of Five Thousand." A friend of his wrote and asked him that spring how his cattle were doing. For answer Charlie painted that picture of a dying cow and sent it to him.

In July we were working on the Maginnis' range, gathering up what cattle there was left to move them across the river. It was hard work, and we weren't getting a thing; we'd ride all morning and maybe only find a couple of weak-kneed, gaunted steers, and they were giving us a lot of trouble, because the weaker and poorer cattle are, the harder they are to drive. That country along Box Elder is as flat as the palm of your hand and no shade. The weather was hot, and the dead cattle stunk in the coulees—you'd come across little bunches of ten to fifteen or twenty of them piled up—pfew! I can smell them yet. There was an old fellow working with us who had some cattle on the range; I don't remember his name. But I'll never forget the way he stopped, with the sweat pouring off his face, looked up at the sun, sober as a judge, and asked, "Where the hell was you last January?"

The blizzards dealt a crushing blow to the industry. Ranchers went into bankruptcy. The Cheyenne Club defaulted on its bonds and sold out for 20 cents on the dollar. The St. Louis shoe company that had bought a great herd worth over a quarter of a million dollars sold out what was left of it to a cowboy for his year's wages.

The outfits that survived realized they could not run such risks again. They must have some means of feeding and sheltering their cattle in an emergency. The bubble had burst and the bonanza was over. It was the end of an era.

LIVE STOCK EXCHANGE.

Rain or Shine

(See Acknowledgments, page 191)

(hum) _____ We're a-

lone Don-ey Gal, in the rain and hail,

driv - ing them dog - ies on __ down the trail. It's

Refrain

rain or shine, sleet or snow,

First time

End

me   and my Don - ey Gal are bound   to go.   A   go

We're alone Doney Gal, in the rain and the hail
Drivin' them dogies on down the trail.

REFRAIN:
It's rain or shine, sleet or snow
Me and my Doney Gal are bound to go!

A cowboy's life is a wearisome thing,
It's rope and brand and ride and sing.

REFRAIN

We ride the range from sun to sun,
For a cowboy's work, Lord, is never done.

REFRAIN

He's up and gone at the break of day,
Driving them dogies all on their way.

REFRAIN

We're alone Doney Gal, in the rain and the hail
Drivin' them dogies on down the trail.

THE CONFLICT OF RANCHER
AND SETTLER

The blizzards of 1886 and 1887, after which many of the big ranching companies went bankrupt, speeded up changes then taking place that would put an end to the Cattle Kingdom and the era of the open range forever.

Free grazing lands, unfenced and of almost boundless extent, had made the fortunes of the cattlemen. These grazing lands of the High Plains were *public domain;* that is, they were the property of the nation, of the American people and its government. They had been taken, true enough, by force of war and conquest from the Indian peoples, but as of 1890 they were not yet privately owned by any individual, company, corporation, or state.

And yet, ever since the Civil War, settlers had been moving out onto the grazing lands in a steady stream, fencing off plots and filing claims for them with the Federal Government. These people filed their claims under the Homestead Act of 1862, which had been passed to promote farm settlement in the West, and to give war veterans especially a chance to get land cheaply, and to own it. Under the Homestead Act any citizen over 21 years could lay a claim to 160 acres of the public domain. If he lived on the land for five years—thus proving good faith—and built a house, put up fences, and so on, then the land became his property.

There were all kinds of people among the homesteaders besides veterans. Some were farmers from the East, some were European immigrants. Some were cowboys who had lost their jobs during the hard times of 1886–1887, and who now turned to farming to make a living. The pace of settlement quickened during the 1880's thanks to the promotional activities of the railroads, which had lands to sell on both sides of their tracks. New technological developments, like wind-driven water pumps and barbed wire to fence in the stock instead of rail fences, were also an important aid to settlement on the high grasslands where both wood and water were scarce.

A few of the big ranches had survived the blizzards; some of them, as a matter of fact, had even managed to prosper during the hard years. Their owners were not pleased with the advance of small farmers onto the Plains. Years of uninterrupted use of the public domain had given them the feeling that this land was theirs. The grasslands were cattle lands: couldn't the blue-nosed nesters understand that?

In many parts of the range country during the late 1870's and the 1880's, conflicts between ranchers and settlers were frequent, bloody, and brutal. In Texas, for example, there was the Lincoln County War of 1878; in Montana, in 1882–1883, a group of big stockmen calling themselves The Stranglers rounded up settlers, accused

Homesteaders.

them of rustling cattle, and hung fifty or sixty of them
without the formality of a trial.

The most deliberate and organized effort to check the
advance of the settlers by terrorist means took place in
Johnson County, northern Wyoming, in 1892. This was
the final effort to keep the open range unsettled; like all
other efforts it failed. But the Johnson County War provides a dramatic picture of the lawless brutality that accompanied the end of the cowboy era and the open
range.

Much of our knowledge of this war comes from *Banditti of the Plains* by Asa Shinn Mercer, who was a champion of the settlers and small ranchmen. His book, published in 1894, was almost immediately suppressed by a
court injunction secured by the cattle kings. The plates
were destroyed and Mercer was jailed for sending ob-
scene material through the mails. The entire edition of
the book, except for a few hundred copies that were
smuggled out of the warehouse, was seized and burned.

In his work Mercer charged that wealthy cattlemen
dominated the state of Wyoming and shaped its law to
suit their own selfish needs. "The livestock industry of
Wyoming," he wrote,

has been the leading pursuit for more than a double dec-
ade of years, and the stockmen have dominated the
political and financial policy of the territory from its
establishment in 1868 down to 1892. The legislature has
always been largely made up of livestock owners or local
representatives of Eastern and foreign cattle syndicates.
In 1872 the Wyoming Stock Growers' Association organized, the membership comprising most of the leading

The chuck wagon.

stock growers of the commonwealth. . . . This body was a strong, centralized power, and for years virtually shaped the territorial policy. . . . The stock-growing industry was in full command of the law-making department. Naturally they dominated everywhere. The people acquiesced because of the magnitude of the cattle interests.

The stockmen first of all harassed the settlers by charging that they were rustlers and hauling them into court as cattle thieves. But public opinion was on the side of the settlers, and juries would not convict. And so the big ranchers tried another way. They secured the passage of the Maverick Bill which made the branding of any unbranded calf by anyone not a member of the Stock Growers' Association a felony. This meant that small ranchers and settlers could not round up their own animals and brand them without being charged with a crime and having their cattle taken away and sold for the benefit of the Association.

In Johnson County the Stock Growers' Association went to work to enforce the law under the leadership of Fred Canton, their chief range inspector and deputy United States marshal. Association inspectors at markets and shipping terminals seized all cattle not bearing approved brands. In ten months they had impounded 16,000 cattle, and of these they sold 5,000, withholding the proceeds from the proper owners.

A great outcry arose in the state. Newspapers attacked the cattle kings for their high-handed ways and their lawlessness. Violence followed. In the summer of 1889 two settlers on the Sweetwater River in Carbon County, James Averill and Ella Watson, were lynched; the murder

Lynching in Cañon City, Colorado, 1888.

was instigated, it was widely believed, by a big cattleman named Bothwell. A reporter described the scene when people from Casper found the bodies two days later:

Hanging from the limb of a stunted pine growing on the summit of a cliff fronting the Sweetwater River were the bodies of James Averill and Ella Watson. Side by side they swung, their faces swollen and discolored almost beyond recognition. Common cowboy lariats had been used and both had died by strangulation, neither having fallen over two feet. Judging from signs too plain to be mistaken, a desperate struggle had taken place on the cliff, and both man and woman had fought for their lives until the last.

As for the land of the dead settlers, it ended up as the property of Bothwell, and part of his ranch. The big rancher converted Ella's cabin into an ice-house. But terror of this type enraged the settlers rather than frightened them. They became more united and more determined than ever to fight the big cattlemen. And so violence became the order of the day in Wyoming.

In November of 1891 four men, including the Stock Growers' agent, Fred Canton, made a dawn attack on a cabin on Powder River. They had come to hang two cowboys turned homesteader, Nate Champion and Ross Gilbertson. Mercer describes the scene:

As the door swung open it stood against the foot of the bed occupied by Champion. With pistols pointed, one of the [raiding] party said, "Give up! We've got you this time," and immediately fired at Champion. The latter seized his revolver from under his pillow and com-

menced shooting, whereupon the would-be murderers escaped from the house. The blood at the door, the gun, clothing and horses left near the cabin not only evidenced the fact of some effective shooting on the part of Champion, but gave identification as to the assaulters.

Nate Champion now became a leader of the settlers. He was a Texan, a soft-spoken, fine-looking man with a sweeping brown mustache. As a cowboy he had worked for big outfits and drawn good pay, but had been laid off after the blizzards. The cattle kings accused him of belonging to the Red Sash gang, a bunch of rustlers, but they had never brought this charge against him so long as he worked for them.

In December, 1891, violence struck again on the outskirts of Buffalo, the only town in Johnson county. Two homesteaders were shot in the back as they drove home from town with their winter supplies. Now the settlers cried out for revenge against the cattle barons: raid their stock, burn their ranches, they demanded. But Red Angus, the Johnson County sheriff, would have none of such talk. The settlers, he said, should not act outside the law or resort to violence.

But the Wyoming Stock Growers' Association was planning to do exactly that. They had in mind nothing less than a full-scale invasion of Johnson County. Calling themselves The Regulators, they formed a secret society and raised money from Association members. Tom Smith was sent down to Texas to hire twenty-five gunfighters and bring them north; the pay for these mercenaries was $150 a month, plus a bounty of $50 for each man killed.

Homesteaders cutting through cattlemen's wire fences, Custer County, Nebraska, 1885.

The Regulators' expedition to Johnson County was to be headed by Frank E. Wolcott, the manager of a large ranch and a one-time major in the U.S. Army, and George W. Baxter, general manager of the Western Union Beef Company and a former governor of the state. Mercer sketched the plan of campaign

to go direct to Buffalo, kill Sheriff Angus and his deputies, and there be reinforced with a large number of co-workers; when they would capture the town, kill twenty or thirty citizens and then raid the settlements in the county, killing or driving out several hundred more, thus getting rid of all their enemies.

This objective accomplished, thought Mercer, there would be similar forays into Natrona, Converse, and Weston Counties. The result would be a general reign of terror in northern Wyoming: "Hundreds of settlers would gather up their families and fly for safety."

On April 6, 1892, a train with six cars pulled into Cheyenne from Denver. Three cars were loaded with horses; two held ammunition, dynamite, wagons, camping supplies, rations, and a case of Winchester rifles. One car carried the twenty-five gun-fighters from Texas; they were joined at Denver by twenty-five Wyoming Regulators—ranch managers and foremen, Association detectives and inspectors. There were also two "war" correspondents along.

Fred Canton was on the train, carrying a death list— the names of the men marked for destruction, starting with Sheriff Red Angus and including Nate Champion and sixty others. He and his band made a fast run to

Casper, which they reached before dawn on the morning of April 7. There the wagons were unloaded; the horsemen mounted up, and the cavalcade moved off across the open prairie toward Buffalo. Tom Smith had promised the Texans that they would be met by a crowd of Wyoming and Dakota cowboys, but not one cowboy from these states showed up to take part in the "war."

On April 8, Wolcott received news that made him change his plans. Baxter's foreman rode in with the news that Nate Champion and Nick Ray, a homesteader, were wintering at an old line camp, the K.C. The Regulators decided to swing over to the camp, wipe out Champion and Ray, and then move on toward Buffalo.

On April 9 the Regulators surrounded Nate Champion's cabin at daybreak, and waited. "In a little while," Mercer tells us,

Nick Ray came out of the house and walked several steps from the door when he was shot and felled to the ground. Champion rushed to the door, gun in hand, and poured a volley at the besiegers, all the time a hot fire being directed at him. He closed the door and evidently watched from the window whence he could see that his friend Ray was slowly crawling toward the door. When Ray was close to the step, Champion opened the door, sent another volley toward the stables and creek, then laid down his gun and, with bullets thick as hail flying around him, stepped out and dragged his friend into the house.

In between the action Nate managed to write an account of his ordeal in a little memo book, setting down, in this extraordinary document, exactly what was taking place.

Me and Nick were getting breakfast when the attack took place. Two men here with us—Bill Jones and another man. The old man went out after water and did not come back. His friend went out to see what was the matter and he did not come back. Nick started out and I told him to look out, that I thought there was someone in the stable and would not let them come back. Nick is shot, but not dead yet. He is awful sick. I must go and wait on him.

It is now about two hours since the first shot. Nick is still alive.

Canton and Wolcott were uneasy over the delay; they were due that very night in Buffalo, sixty miles away, to launch a coordinated attack with their men who were already spotted throughout the town. They kept up a steady fire against the cabin.

Champion's story continues.

They are still shooting and are all around the house. Boys, there is bullets coming in like hail. The fellows is in such shape, I can't get at them. They are shooting from stable and river and back of the house.

Nick is dead. He died about 9 o'clock. I see a smoke down at the stable. I think they have fired it. I don't think they intend to let me get away this time.

It is now about noon. There is someone at the stable yet; they are throwing a rope out at the door and drawing it back. I guess it is to draw me out. I wish that duck would get out further so I could get a shot at him.

By early afternoon the firing had died down. Then, about 3 o'clock, a boy driving a wagon with a man on horseback behind him passed along the road. The man was Black Jack Flagg, like Champion a former cowboy and a leader of the settlers; he too was on Canton's death list.

Flagg saw the men around the cabin and at once realized what was up. He whipped his horse back to the wagon and cut the team loose. The boy mounted one of the horses and galloped off over the ridge. He and Flagg soon escaped the Regulators after a mad chase across country.

Meantime Champion was writing in his diary:

Boys, I feel pretty lonesome just now. I wish there was someone here with me so we could watch all sides at once. . . . It's about 3 o'clock now. There was a man in a buckboard and one on horseback just passed. They fired on them as they went by. I don't know if they killed them or not. I seen lots of men come out on horses on the other side of the river and take after them. I shot at the men in the stable just now; don't know if I got any or not.

Wolcott and Canton knew that Flagg would rouse the whole countryside; men would be out in force to oppose them now that their surprise was gone. They decided to fire the cabin. Flagg's wagon was dragged up, piled high with pine knots and brush, and pushed up against the ouside wall.

With the flames roaring around outside Champion wrote the last words in his diary:

It's not night yet. The house is all fired.
Goodbye, boys, if I never see you again.

NATHAN D. CHAMPION

Putting the little book in his vest pocket and holding his Winchester in his hand, Nate leaped out the window and darted toward a nearby ravine.

What happened next is described by Sam T. Clover, correspondent for the *Chicago Herald,* and one of the "war" correspondents with the Regulators:

The roof of the cabin was the first to catch on fire, spreading rapidly downward until the north wall was a sheet of flames. Volumes of smoke poured in at the open window from the burning wagon, and in a short time through the plastered cracks of the log house puffs of smoke worked outwards. Still the doomed man remained doggedly concealed. . . . "Reckon the cuss has shot himself," remarked one of the waiting marksmen. "No fellow could stay in that hole a minute and be alive."

These words were barely spoken when there was a shout, "There he goes!" and a man clad in his stocking feet, bearing a Winchester in his hands and a revolver in his belt, emerged from a volume of black smoke that issued from the rear door of the house and started off across the open space surrounding the cabin into a ravine, fifty yards south of the house. But the poor devil jumped square into the arms of two of the best shots in the outfit, who stood with levelled Winchesters around the bend waiting for his appearance.

Champion saw them too late, for he overshot his mark just as a bullet struck his rifle arm, causing the gun to fall from his nerveless grasp. Before he could draw his revolver a second shot struck him in the breast and a third and fourth found their way to his heart.

Nate Champion, the king of cattle thieves, and the bravest man in Johnson County, was dead.

For a long time the Regulators stood around the bullet-ridden body, gazing down in mingled awe and admiration at this one man who had held off fifty. Said Major Wolcott, "By God, if I had fifty men like you, I could whip the whole state of Wyoming!"

Nate's little memo book was found and passed around, then thrown back upon the body. Sam Clover picked it up and pocketed it. Nate's entire account of the shoot-out appeared later on the front page of the *Chicago Herald*.

The Regulators dragged Nick Ray's charred body out of the smouldering ruins of the cabin, and laid it aside Nate's. A sign, CATTLE THIEVES BEWARE, was pinned to Champion's shirt. Two names were crossed off the death list. Wolcott's men moved off toward Buffalo.

But the people of Buffalo had been alerted by Flagg. Robert Foote, leading merchant of the town, galloped up and down the streets calling the people to arms like a western Paul Revere:

Wyoming has been invaded! An armed body of assassins has entered our country and with bullet and fire has destroyed the lives and property of our people. This same murderous gang is now marching on our village . . . to murder our citizens and destroy our property. As men and fellow citizens who love your homes, your wives and your children, I call upon you to shoulder your arms and come to the front to protect all that you hold dear against this approaching foe. If you have no arms come to my store and get them free of charge.

Sheriff Red Angus marched out at the head of a large body of citizens. Regulator scouts brought in to Wolcott the news that the way to Buffalo was blocked. So the invaders turned back and rode to the TA Ranch on Crazy Woman Creek, about fourteen miles from Buffalo. There they built barricades, dug trenches, and prepared for a siege.

By daylight on April 11, three or four hundred Johnson County people had surrounded the ranch—small ranchers, cowboys, settlers, and townspeople. And still they streamed in, furious at the news of Champion's death and burning for revenge.

The battle went on for two days. Regulator ammunition and supplies were running out, but the Regulators had succeeded in sending word of their plight back to Cheyenne. There Governor Barber sent telegram after telegram to Washington, urging the President of the United States to send Federal troops to the relief of the Regulators. "I have," responded President Harrison,

in compliance with your call for aid of the United States forces to protect the state of Wyoming against domestic violence, ordered the Secretary of War to concentrate a sufficient force at the scene of the disturbance and to cooperate with your authorities.

On the afternoon of April 12 a bugle call sounded over the hills. Riding to the rescue came Troops C, D, and E of the Black Sixth Cavalry Regiment under Colonel J. J. Van Horn. Then the Regulators surrendered to the Federal authorities and were escorted by the troops to Fort McKinney.

But none of the Regulators was ever brought to court to answer for his crimes, and no one was punished for the murder of Champion and Ray. In January of 1893 the hired gunmen were sent back to Texas.

In Buffalo, Nick and Nate received the funeral honors due heroes. "These men," said Reverend Rader, "were not criminals. They were of Christian parents. Ray leaves five brothers and three sisters. His parents could not be notified as the wires were cut." Then the procession moved up Main Street and out to the town cemetery. Hundreds of people followed the bodies on foot; 150 mounted men brought up the rear of the cortege.

The Ballad of Nate Champion

It was a little blood-stained book which a bullet had torn in twain.
It told the fate of Nick and Nate, which is known to all of you;
He had the nerve to write it down while the bullets fell like rain.
At your request, I'll do my best to read those lines again.

"Two men stayed with us here last night, Bill Jones and another man,
Went to the river, took a pail, will come back if they can.

I told old Nick not to look out, there might be someone
    near,
He opened the door; shot to the floor, he'll never live, I fear.

Two hours since the shots began, the bullets thick as hail!
Must wait on Nick, he's awful sick, he's still alive but pale.
At stable, river and back of me, men are sending lead.
I cannot get a shot to hit, it's nine and Nick is dead.

Down at the stable I see a smoke, I guess they'll burn the
    hay.
From what I've seen they do not mean for me to get away.
It's now about noon, I see a rope thrown in and out the door.
I wish that duck would show his pluck, he'd use a gun no
    more.

I don't know what has become of the boys that stayed with
    us last night.
Just two or more boys with me and we would guard the
    cabin right.
I'm lonesome, boys, it's two o'clock, two men just come in
    view,
And riding fast, as they went past, were shot at by the crew.

I shot a man down in the barn, don't know if I hit or not.
Must look again, I see someone, it looks like there's a blot.
I hope they did not get those men that across the bridge did
    run.
If I had a pair of glasses here, I think I'd know someone.

They're just through shelling the house, I hear the splitting
    wood;
And I guess they'll light the house tonight, and burn me out
    for good.

I'll have to leave when night comes on, they'll burn me if I
    stay;
I guess I'll make a running break and try to get away.

They've shot another volley in, but to burn me is their game,
And as I write, it's not yet night, and the house is all aflame.
So good-bye boys, if I get shot, I got to make a run,
So on this leaf I'll sign my name, Nathan D. Champion."

The light is out, the curtain drawn, the last sad act is played.
You know the fate that met poor Nate, and of the run he
    made.
And now across the Big Divide, and at the Home Ranch door
I know he'll meet and warmly greet the boys that went
    before.

10

THE WORKING COWBOY

Cowboys, at first, were mainly Texans, veterans, black men, and Mexicans. As ranching spread over the range, the ranks were swelled by men from every part of the United States as well as from abroad. Rich and poor, city boys and farm boys, millionaires' sons, they came from various professions and from no profession at all.

The typical cowboy was a young man between the ages of 17 and 28. Cowpunching was a strenuous calling to grow old in, and yet some did follow it into their middle years.

As early as the 1860's, playing at cowboy was becoming a popular children's game. The *Galveston News* of August 16, 1866, noted that

The little children, as early as they can walk, pilfer their mother's tape and make lassos to rope the kittens and the ducks. The boys, as soon as they can climb on a pony, are off to the prairie to drive stock. As they advance toward manhood, their highest ambition is to conquer a pitching mustang or throw a wild bull by the tail.

In these years the lure of the trail was capturing the

imagination of adventurous youth. W. B. Harderman, of Devine, Texas, recalled how it all began for him:

I was just a farmer boy, started to church at Prairie Lea one Sunday, met Tom Baylor (he having written me a note several days before, asking if I wanted to go up the trail), and the first thing he said was, "Well, are you going?" I said "Yes," so he said, "Well, you have no time to go to church." . . . There I was, with a white shirt, collar and cravat, starting on the trail. You can imagine how green I was.

High-spirited, healthy, and vigorous, a cowpuncher would try anything once. If a problem could be solved by action he acted fast. If he could do nothing about a situation he accepted it without complaining. Jim Flood, foreman of Andy Adams' outfit, on hearing that hostile Indians might be ahead, said:

So, boys, if we're ever to see the Blackfoot Agency, there's but one course for us to take, and that's straight ahead. As old Oliver Loring, the first Texas cowman that ever drove a herd, used to say, "Never borrow trouble or cross a river before you reach it." So when the cattle are through grazing, let them hit the trail north. It's entirely too late for us to veer away from any Indians.

The cowboy was used to hardship; he joked about it and made light of it. Teddy Blue gave this description of his comrades:

They were intensely loyal to the outfit they were working for and would fight to the death for it. They would follow their wagon boss through hell and never com-

Drunken cowboy.

plain. I have seen them ride into camp after two days and nights on herd, lay down on their saddle blankets in the rain and sleep like dead men. They got up laughing and joking about some good time they had had in Ogallala or Dodge City.

As for a cowboy's personal life, it was nobody's business but his own. Too much curiosity about others was not a healthy thing.

A man might tell as much or as little about himself as he saw fit, or nothing at all. Nobody cared. All that was required of him was to do his work faithfully, and not to disturb the peace and harmony of the outfit by ill-temper or viciousness. These men might live together and work together season after season, year after year, without knowing anything about each other personally other than the names they went by.

There were many like Jim Culver, who arrived at the Lang ranchhouse more dead than alive after an adventure in the icy waters of the Little Missouri. Lang liked him and hired him. He was a young man of about twenty, fearless, of good morals, and with an unusual amount of energy and initiative. When a mean horse side-flopped and killed him two years later, all that was known about him was—"He said his name was Jim Culver."

Nicknames were the rule in the West and were given in accordance with a man's characteristics, looks, or habits—for example, Gloomy Thompson, Sudden Lucas, Horse-face Bill, Fatty Hamilton, Lazy Dick, Itchy Jake, and Vinegar Hall. The cowboy's speech, in general, was rich in humor and spiced with quaint phraseology. Of a bald-headed cook it was said, "He ain't got any hair 'tween him and heaven." A grafter was so crooked he "could swallow nails an' spit out corkscrews." A no-good man "wasn't worth a barrel of shucks."

Blacks and Mexicans were an important element in the ranks of the cowboys. It has been estimated that of the 35,000 men who went up the trails from 1865 to 1895, at least 5,000 were black. Black cowboys did all the jobs that white cowboys did.

Some died in stampedes, some froze to death, some drowned. Some were too slow with guns, some too fast. . . . They numbered thousands, among them many of the best riders, ropers and wranglers. They hunted wild horses and wolves, and a few of them hunted men. Some were villains, some were heroes.

Most of the black cowboys had been born slaves and raised on ranches. When the Civil War was over they joined outfits and went up the trail. But few black cowpunchers ever rose to be foremen, for white southerners would not take orders from a black man.

Perhaps the most famous black cowboy was Nat Love. Born a slave in 1854 in a Tennessee cabin, Love left for Kansas after the Civil War, at the age of fifteen. Reaching Dodge City, he became a cowboy and remained one until 1890. Then when cowboy jobs became scarce, he took a job as a Pullman porter. In his autobiography Love told how he first became a cowhand.

Approaching a party who were eating their breakfast, I got to speak with them. They asked me to have some breakfast with them, which invitation I gladly accepted.

They proved to be a Texas outfit who had just come up with a herd of cattle and having delivered them, were preparing to return. There were several colored cowboys among them, and good ones too. After breakfast I asked the camp boss for a job as a cowboy. He asked if I could ride a wild horse. I said, "Yes, sir," He said "If you can, I will give you a job."

So he spoke to one of the colored cowboys called Bronko Jim, and told him to go out and rope old Good Eye, saddle him and put me on his back. Bronko Jim gave me a few pointers and told me to look out, for the horse was especially bad on pitching. I told Jim I was a good rider and not afraid of him; I thought I had rode pitching horses before, but from the moment I mounted Good Eye I knew I had not learned what pitching was. This proved the worst horse to ride I had ever mounted in my life, but I stayed with him and the cowboys were the most surprised outfit you ever saw, as they had taken me for a tenderfoot, pure and simple.

After the horse got tired and I dismounted the boss said he would give me a job and pay me $30.00 a month and more later on. He asked what my name was and I answered Nat Love. He said to the boys "We will call him Red River Dick." I went by that name for a long time.

Love was a champion cowboy. It was his great skill as a horseman that earned him the nickname, Deadwood Dick, when the outfit arrived in Deadwood at the end of a drive.

The next morning, July 4th, the gambler and mining

Nat Love.

men made up a purse of $200 for a roping contest between the cowboys that were then in town. It did not take long to arrange the details for the contest and contestants, six of them being colored cowboys, including myself. Our trail boss was chosen and he picked out twelve of the most wild and vicious horses that he could find.

The conditions of the contest were that each of us who were mounted was to rope, throw, tie, bridle and saddle, and mount the particular horse picked for us in the shortest time possible. The man accomplishing the feat in the quickest time to be declared the winner. It seems to me that the horse chosen for me was the most vicious of the lot. Everything being in readiness, the "45" cracked and we all sprang forward together, each of us making for our particular mustang.

I roped, threw, tied, bridled, saddled, and mounted my mustang in exactly nine minutes from the crack of the gun. The time of the next nearest competitor was twelve minutes and thirty seconds. This gave me the record and championship of the West, which I held up to the time I quit the business in 1890, and my record has never been beaten. Right there the assembled crowd named me Deadwood Dick and proclaimed me champion roper of the western cattle country.

Mexican cowboys had a great influence on the clothing and equipment that North American cowboys used. The Stetson hat evolved from the Spanish and Mexican sombrero; the broad brim kept sand, dirt, and mud from flying in the cowboy's eyes. The hat was used to dip water, to fan a fire, and as a pillow. The Stetson, so cowboys claimed, never wore out and always held its shape.

The bandana was worn knotted loosely around the neck, giving protection from sun and windburn. When riding the drag, the cowpuncher used the bandana to cover his face and to keep dust out of his mouth, nose, and lungs. It was also used as a towel, tourniquet, and sling.

The cowboy's shirt was of brightly colored flannel with long sleeves buttoned at the wrist, and it was often covered by a loose vest that contained a pocket for tobacco, cigarette papers, and matches. His tight-fitting trousers were usually made of heavy blue denim, and the trouser legs were stuffed into his boots. Neither belt nor suspenders were worn. Tied behind the saddle was a waterproof slicker like a fisherman's oilskin.

The cowpuncher wore high, sharp-heeled boots made of calfskin. The heels enabled the cowpuncher to dig in and brake when roping from the ground, and they also stopped the rider's foot from slipping through the stirrup on a bucking horse. Gloves or gauntlets with large cuffs to protect hands and wrists from burns and blisters completed the outfit.

Saddles might look alike, but they differed from each other as much as one pair of shoes differs from another. Once a cowboy had broken in his saddle he could not be persuaded to loan it or part with it.

"I wouldn't ride a mile in that thing o' yourn for the best heifer that runs the range," says the cowpuncher, referring contemptuously to the prized saddle of another. "I'd plum have a misery if I had to ride yourn," is the answer.

A saddle might be more expensive than a horse, depending upon the amount of leather tooling and silver decoration. One song goes:

Oh a ten dollar hoss and a forty dollar saddle,
And I'm riding out to punch in Texas cattle.

A cowboy felt naked without his Colt six-shooter. He always removed his gun before entering another's house or when sitting at his own table. The pistol belt was worn loose; the weight of the weapon fell upon the thigh.

A horse, for the cowboy, was an instrument of work. It was also a means of transportation, often the difference between life and death, and a deep friend. Without a horse to carry him the vast distances over the prairies, a man was helpless. A horse thief was hated and when captured was quickly executed.

Cowboys had to be good riders, for riding was their business. They loved to boast of the tough horses they had mounted and the wild rides they had had. A cowboy might brag that he could "ride anything that wears hair." One puncher, describing one such wild ride, said:

He went into the air, struck the bridle with his front feet and knocked it off. He then swallowed his neck up to his shoulders and proceeded on up to where the lights of Jerusalem shone. There we parted company and the bronc come down alone.

Andy Adams recalled the end of the long drive to Montana, and the rough time he had when the trip was over and the horses he had come to love so well had to be abandoned.

At no time in my life, before or since, have I felt so keenly the parting between man and horse as I did that September evening in Montana. For on the trail an affection springs up between a man and his mount which is almost human. Every privation which he endures, his horse endures with him—carrying him through falling weather, swimming rivers by day and riding in the lead of stampedes by night, always faithful, always willing, and always patiently enduring every hardship, from exhausting hours under saddle to the sufferings of a dry drive.

Now, when the trail is a lost occupation and reverie, and reminiscences carry the mind back to that day, there are friends and faces that may be forgotten, but there are horses that never will be. There were emergencies in which the horse was everything, his rider merely the accessory. But together, man and horse, they were the force that made it possible to move the millions of cattle which passed up and over the various trails of the west.

Black Jack Davy

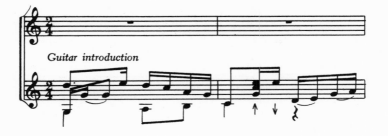

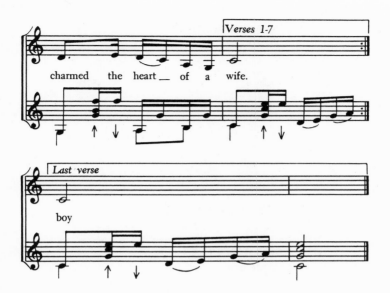

charmed the heart of a wife.

boy

Black Jack Davy come a-riding through the woods,
Singing a song so gaily,
He sang so loud made the wild wood ring,
Charmed the heart of a lady,
Charmed the heart of a wife.

She put on her fine Sunday shoes,
All made of Spanish leather,
He put on his old cork boots,
And they both rode off together
The lady and Black Jack boy.

My lord he came home that night,
Inquiring for his lady,
Servant spoke before she thought,
"She's gone with the Black Jack Davy,
She's gone with the Black Jack boy."

"Go saddle me up my best black mare,
The gray is ne'er so speedy,
For I'll ride all night, and I'll ride all day,
Till I overtake my lady,
Till I overtake my wife."

He rode all night till the midnight moon,
He came to the edges of the water,
There he saw the gypsies' fire,
Sound of his lady singing,
The song of the Black Jack boy.

"Will you forsake your house and home,
Will you forsake your baby?
Will you forsake your husband too,
To go with the Black Jack Davy,
To go with the gypsy boy?"

"Yes, I'll forsake my house and home,
And I'll forsake my baby,
And I'll forsake my husband too,
To go with the gypsy Davy,
To go with the Black Jack boy."

"Last night I slept in a feather bed,
Sheets turned down so bravely,
Tonight I'll sleep in the mud and the rain,
By the side of Black Jack Davy,
By the side of the Black Jack boy."

Cowboys crooned to the cattle at night to lull them to sleep. They also sang to their horses, talking to them about the suffering in life as they might to no other living soul. Sometimes it seemed as though the horse listened to every word, and understood.

Poor Lonesome Cowboy

I'm a poor lone - some cow - boy. I'm a

2nd voice or instrument

poor lone - some cow - boy. I'm a

poor lone - some cow - boy, and a

long _____ ways from home.

I'm a poor lonesome cowboy (3 times)
And a long way from home.

I ain't got no father
To buy the clothes I wear.

I ain't got no mother
To mend the clothes I wear.

I ain't got no brother
To drive the steers with me.

I ain't got no sweetheart
To sit and talk with me.

I'm a poor lonesome cowboy
And a long way from home.

CONCLUSION

A hundred years after their beginning, the Cattle Kingdom and the cowboy still cast their magical spell. Although lasting only three decades, the life of the cowboy caught the world's imagination. All over the globe, children still play at cowboys and Indians and adults flock to movies with western themes.

The Cattle Kingdom arose after the Civil War out of the necessity of meeting the demands of the growing industrial system of the East. Workers needed cheap meat. On the western plains, the cowboy and his Texas longhorns supplied this need.

When the war ended, Texas was bursting with cattle, but there was no market for them in the impoverished and war-torn South. Rounding up their nervous, bony cattle, the Texas ranchers marched them northward to the railroads advancing westward across Kansas. The steers were shipped to Chicago and Kansas City to be slaughtered and made into meat for the Eastern worker's table.

This movement of cattle across half a continent was a huge operation: it meant the extinction of the sixty million buffalo on the High Plains and spelled the doom of the Plains Indians' way of life. The Great Plains—once considered the Great American Desert, reserved forever as the home of the Indian and the buffalo—were conquered and plundered. The primeval ecology of the Plains was destroyed and the buffalo were replaced by domestic cattle. The slaughter of the buffalo was encouraged by the American government, since it undermined the Indian way of life and helped end the Indian resistance to the white man's encroachment.

In its turn, the era of the cattlemen and the open range was ended by the settlement on the Plains of farmers who plowed up and fenced off the land, barring it to huge herds of cattle. Much of this land was not suitable for farming because of the harsh extremes of weather and the lack of water. Many of the settlers suffered cruelly and had to abandon their farms. The wilderness, with its wildlife and its natural grasses and wildflowers, was destroyed along with its Indian culture. What kind of progress was achieved by this destruction and what price did the American people pay for it? Was the progress worth the price?

The first cowboys were mainly Texans and the cattle business was carried on by small local ranches. But in the 1880's, as the demand for meat swelled and profits increased, cattle raising turned into a vast, speculative enterprise. People from all walks of life and from many countries, anxious for quick profits, invested their money in ranches and cattle companies. Fortunes were made and lost from the buying and selling of herds that the owners had probably never even seen.

The vastness of the Great Plains and the freedom and adventure of a cowboy's life stirred the imaginations of young men in Texas and throughout the country. Before the Civil War, in the same way, thousands of young men had been lured to the sea by its promise of mystery, beauty, and romance. The majority of the cowboys were sons of small farmers and settlers, ex-slaves, and Mexicans. The myth of the cowpuncher shows him all in his glory riding across the plains with his high-spirited horse, six-gun, lariat, and wide-brimmed Stetson to rescue the rancher's beautiful daughter. In reality he was a working man whose whole life and existence were bounded and taken up with the care of cattle and who seldom saw any woman or damsel in distress.

The trail was the college of the cowboy. In all of the West there was no wilder or rougher school. Cowboys who went up the trail were looked upon as heroes and every young boy's ambition was to make such a trip. The trail created the cowboy and drew him to national attention. In later life those who had been through it looked back with regret to a memory of brotherhood and joy forever lost.

The cowboy experience began in 1866 and was over and gone forever by 1890, brought to an end by overgrazing and overstocking and the coming of the farmer to the Plains. The tragic blizzards of 1886–1887 proved that cattle could not just be turned loose upon the High Plains to care for themselves. Ranchers would have to buy land from the government, fence it in, and provide feed for the winter if the cattle were to survive. Stockmen would have to share the land with wheat farmers moving west in response to free and cheap government and railroad-promotion land.

The cowboy epic arose during the Gilded Age and was

a part of the titanic achievement of the American people in the construction of an industrial empire. By contrast to the Gilded Age with its greed and imprisonment of people in slums and factories, the cowboy appeared as a free and heroic personality choosing his own destiny. This image survives today as a myth that veils from American minds the more repulsive features of an age that turned men into machines, exploited them cruelly, and destroyed the spirit of democratic equality in a brazenly class-oriented society. The cowboy contributed much to the wealth of the Gilded Age, but he did not himself grow wealthy. In this respect his experience was typical of most ordinary American workers of that time.

THE END

SONG NOTES

The guitar accompaniments to these songs have been composed by John Anthony Scott, Robert Alan Scott, and Kent Sidon. They are designed for the repertoire of the elementary and intermediate student of the classical guitar. Copyright by John Anthony Scott.

I Ride an Old Paint

This song comes from Margaret Larkin of New Mexico, whose exquisite collection, *Singing Cowboy*, was first published by Alfred A. Knopf in 1931. Carl Sandburg, that great folklorist, thought of it as one of the most fascinating cowboy songs.

The Sprig of Thyme

This is a Texas version of an ancient British love-lament, and was provided by Mrs. Sarah Cleveland of Hudson Falls, New York. A Scottish variant of the song contains the following verse:

> Woman is a branchy tree,
> And man a singing wind;
> And in the branches carelessly
> He takes what he can find, find,
> He takes what he can find.

Down by the Brazos

This sings of the rivers of Texas and the sorrows of love. No one seems to remember the name of the cowboy who composed it. We learned it from Alan Lomax.

Colorado Trail

A doctor in a Minnesota hospital learned this song from a cowboy patient who sang it over and over. Carl Sandburg first published it in 1927 in his *American Songbag*.

The Night Herding Song

A cowboy by the name of Harry Stephens composed this lullaby. John A. Lomax first published it in 1910 in his pioneer collection, *Cowboy Songs*.

Git Along Little Dogies

This is one of the oldest Texas trail songs, adapted directly from a Boston-Irish lullaby, "The Boy Who was Taken." For the Irish lyrics, see John A. Scott. ed., *Living Documents* (New York: Washington Square Press, 1969), II, 281.

The Cowboy's Lament

Here is a profound and moving variant of the too-familiar "Streets of Laredo," for which we are indebted to John A. Lomax.

Goodbye Old Paint

This was one of the most popular cowboy songs. Sing whatever words you want and go jogging (or dancing) on forever.

Rain or Shine (Doney Gal)

This comes from Mrs. Louise Henson of San Antonio, Texas, and was first published in 1910 in *Cowboy Songs*.

Black Jack Davy

This is a Texas version of the beautiful old British ballad "The Gypsy Laddie" (Child Collection #200). Texans had a special liking for a song in which even love went on horseback.

Poor Lonesome Cowboy

This song was sung by both English and Mexican buckaroos throughout the West.

ACKNOWLEDGMENTS

Acknowledgment is made to the following for permission to reprint copyrighted material:

Argosy-Antiquarian, Ltd., *Trail Drivers of Texas*, J. M. Hunter, ed., ©
1963; Arno Press, Inc., *The Life and Adventures of Nat Love*, Nat Love
© 1968; Citadel Press, Inc., *The Border and the Buffalo*, John R. Cook,
© 1967; Dodd, Mead & Co., Inc., *The Negro Cowboys*, Philip Durham
and Everett L. Jones, © 1965 by Philip Durham and Everett L. Jones;
Houghton Mifflin Co., *Roosevelt in the Badlands*, Hermann Hagedorn,
© 1921; J. B. Lippincott Co., *Ranching With Roosevelt*, Lincoln A.
Lang, © 1926; Little, Brown & Co., *The Longhorns*, J. Frank Dobie,
© 1941; The Richmond Organization, "Night Herding Song," "Doney
Gal," "The Cowboy's Lament," collected, adapted and arranged by
John A. & Alan Lomax, © 1938, renewed 1966, Ludlow Music, Inc.,
New York and "The Buffalo Skinners," collected, adapted and arranged
by John A. & Alan Lomax, © 1934, renewed 1962, Ludlow Music, Inc.,
New York; University of Oklahoma Press, *We Pointed Them North*,
E. C. Abbott and H. H. Smith, © 1956 and *My Life on the Range*,
John Clay, © 1962; Yale University Press, *Montana: High, Wide, and
Handsome*, Joseph Kinsey Howard, © 1943; and Xerox College Publishing, *The Great Plains*, Walter Prescott Webb, © 1931 by Walter
Prescott Webb, all rights reserved.

Grateful acknowledgment is made for the use of illustrations:

Solomon D. Butcher Collection, Nebraska State Historical Society, 151,
158; Denver Public Library Western Collection, 8, 17, 19, 23, 26, 37, 40,
44, 50, 52, 54, 56, 57, 60, 62, 70, 72, 88, 91, 95, 99, 102, 105, 115, 119,
123, 125, 134, 141, 146, 153, 155, 168, 171, 175, 184; Gilcrease Collection, frontispiece, 35; State Historical Society of Colorado, 76, 85. The
maps in this book are by Edward Malsberg. Special thanks is extended to
Mr. James Davis of the Denver Public Library, Western History Division.

BIBLIOGRAPHY

This bibliography includes some of the main sources used in the preparation of this book, and offers suggestions for further reading on the various topics. All works, unless otherwise stated, are in print at the time of writing (1972).

General

The basic source for the life of the cowboy is J. Marvin Hunter, *Trail Drivers of Texas* (1920; reissued New York: Argosy-Antiquarian, Ltd., 1963, 2 volumes). A number of cowboys have left their reminiscences of life on the trail. Will S. James' *27 Years a Maverick or Life on a Texas Range* (1893; reissued Austin, Texas: Steck-Vaughn Co., Inc. 1968) is well worth reading, as is Charles M. Russell, *Trails Plowed Under* (1927; reissued Garden City, N.Y.: Doubleday & Co., Inc., 1963). The definitive account of life on the trail is Andy Adams, *The Log of a Cowboy* (Boston: Houghton Mifflin Co., 1903; various paperback reissues). See also Charlie Siringo, *A Texas Cowboy or Fifteen Years on the Hurricane Deck of a Spanish Pony* (1885; reissued Lincoln, Nebraska: University of Nebraska Press paperback, 1966).

A number of good secondary sources present an overall view of the open range country and the ranching industry. Edward Everett Dale, *Cow Country* (1924; reissued Norman, Oklahoma: University of Oklahoma Press, 1968) is indispensable. Ernest Osgood, *The Day of the Cattleman* (1929; reissued Chicago:

University of Chicago Press, 1964) is a solidly written book on the open range country from the days of the first Texas drives until 1887. Mari Sandoz, *The Cattlemen: From the Rio Grande Across the Far Marias* (New York: Hastings House, 1958) is a book with a wide sweep, covering the whole story of cattle in North America from the days of Cortes until modern times. Gene Gressley, *Bankers and Cattlemen* (Lincoln: University of Nebraska Press, 1966, hardcover and paper) focuses on the cattle business as an operation financed by absentee owners and financiers in the East.

Many cowboy songs are available in the great collection of John A. and Alan Lomax, *Cowboy Songs and Other Frontier Ballads* (1910; reissued New York: The Macmillan Company, 1938). See also William A. Owens, *Texas Folk Songs* (Austin, Texas: Southern Methodist University Press, 1950; out of print).

Introduction: The Cowboy Myth

Joe B. Frantz and Julian E. Choate, Jr. *The American Cowboy: The Myth and The Reality* (Norman: University of Oklahoma Press, 1955) attempts to explain why the cowboy has become America's most popular folk hero. See also the interesting and detailed studies of legend-making in Kent Ladd Steckmesser, *The Western Hero in History and Legend* (Norman: University of Oklahoma Press, 1965), and Henry Nash Smith's classic *Virgin Land: The American West as Symbol and Myth* (Cambridge, Mass.: Harvard University Press, 1950; reissued in paper by Vintage Books, 1957).

1 and 2: The Great Plains and the Cradle of the Cattle Kingdom

The classic study of the history and ecology of the Great Plains is Walter Prescott Webb, *The Great Plains* (1931; reissued New York: Grosset and Dunlap Universal paperback, 1957). The author provides a detailed bibliography, chapter by chapter, for further exploration of the various phases of the subject. For a fine introduction to the native peoples of the area, see Robert H. Lowie, *Indians of the Plains* (1954; reissued Garden City, N.Y.:

Natural History Press, 1963) and Richard Erdoes, *The Sun Dance People* (New York: Alfred A. Knopf, Inc., 1972; also available as a Vintage Sundial paperback). For the Texas Longhorn, see J. Frank Dobie's superb *The Longhorns* (1941; reissued New York: Grosset and Dunlap Universal paperback, 1957), and *A Vaquero of the Brush Country* (1929; revised and reissued Boston: Little, Brown & Co., 1960).

3: *Abilene and the Chisholm Trail*

The principal source for this chapter was Joseph G. McCoy, *Historic Sketches of the Cattle Trade in the West and Southwest* (1874; reissued Columbus, Ohio: Long's College Book Company, 1951). A good secondary account is Wayne Gard's *The Chisholm Trail* (Norman: University of Oklahoma Press, 1954, 1969).

4: *Up the Trail*

For this chapter see the works by Adams, Siringo, Hunter, and James, cited above. Harry Sinclair Drago, *Great American Cattle Trails: The Story of the Old Cowpaths of the East and the Longhorn Highways of the Plains* (New York: Dodd, Mead & Co., 1965; out of print) relates the story of the cow trails from colonial days until the 1890's.

5: *In Town*

For this chapter see Adams and McCoy, cited above. Also Edward C. Abbott, *We Pointed Them North: Recollections of a Cowpuncher* (1939; reissued Norman: University of Oklahoma Press, 1955, 1966), written with the assistance of Helena Huntington Smith. Highly readable, and a rich source of material is Harry Sinclair Drago's out-of-print *Wild, Wooly and Wicked: The History of the Kansas Cow Town and the Texas Cattle Trade* (New York: Bramhall House, 1960). Robert R. Dykstra, *The Cattle Towns* (New York: Alfred A. Knopf, Inc., 1968; reissued in paper by Atheneum, 1970) is a social history of the Kansas cow towns and railroad shipping terminals.

6: *The Extermination of the Buffalo*

The classic and definitive treatment of the buffalo culture is Tom McHugh's beautifully written *The Time of the Buffalo* (New York: Alfred A. Knopf, Inc., 1972). First-hand accounts of buffalo hunting give the reader an intimate view of life in the High Plains. The native peoples tell their story through their art. See Karen Daniels Petersen, *Plains Indian Art from Fort Marion* (Norman: University of Oklahoma Press, 1971). For contemporary white viewpoints, see the account of a great American anthropologist, Lewis Henry Morgan, *The Indian Journals 1859–62*, Leslie A. White, ed. (Ann Arbor, Mich.: University of Michigan Press, 1959), and Richard Irving Dodge, *The Plains of the Great West* (New York: G. P. Putnam's Sons, 1877; out of print). There have been various secondary accounts of the extinction of the buffalo. Those in print include E. Douglas Branch, *The Hunting of the Buffalo* (1929; reissued Lincoln: University of Nebraska Press, 1962) and Wayne Gard, *The Great Buffalo Hunt* (1959; reissued Lincoln: University of Nebraska Press, 1968).

7: *The Bonanza Years*

James S. Brisbin, *The Beef Bonanza: Or How to Get Rich on the Plains* (1882; reissued Norman: University of Oklahoma Press, 1959) is credited with a major influence in persuading Europeans to invest in the cattle business. Another equally influential book is Walter Baron von Richthofen, *Cattle Raising on the Plains of North America* (1885; reissued Norman: University of Oklahoma Press, 1969). See also Gene Gressley, cited above.

8: *Catastrophe: The Blizzards of 1886 and 1887*

Hermann Hagedorn, *Roosevelt in the Badlands* (Boston: Houghton Mifflin Co., 1921) and Lincoln A. Lang, *Ranching with Roosevelt* (Boston: J. B. Lippincott Co., 1926) give chilling accounts of the winters of 1886 and 1887. Both are out of print.

9: *The Conflict of Rancher and Settler*

The main source for this chapter was Asa S. Mercer, *Banditti of the Plains* (1894; reissued Norman: University of Oklahoma Press, 1954). Mercer's book, written in passion, is biased in favor of the small rancher and the settler. A more scholarly book, Helena Huntington Smith, *The War on Powder River* (Lincoln: University of Nebraska Press, 1967) substantiates Mercer's charges. For the experience of the settler in turning up the sod of the Western Kansas prairie, see John Ise's beautifully written *Sod And Stubble* (1936; reissued Lincoln: University of Nebraska Press, 1967).

10: *The Working Cowboy*

An overall view of the cowpuncher is given in Ramon F. Adams, *The Old-Time Cowhand* (1961; reissued New York: The Macmillan Company, 1968, 1971). For Black buckaroos, see Philip Durham and Everett L. Jones *The Negro Cowboys* (New York: Dodd, Mead & Co., 1965) for a well-documented account of the role that these people played on the open range. Nat Love's *Life and Adventures* (1907; reissued New York: Arno Press, 1968) is a fascinating story of the Western experience of an ex-slave, told in typical Western style.

INDEX

Laurence I. Seidman is a historian and folklorist, with a special interest in the legend and lore of the American West.

He taught for a number of years at the elementary school level, and is now Associate Professor of Education at C.W. Post College. Dr. Seidman is an authority on the use of folk music in the teaching of social studies.

He lives with his family in Great Neck, New York.

John Anthony Scott has taught at Columbia and Amherst colleges and since 1951 has been Chairman of the Department of History at the Fieldston School, New York. He is currently Professor of Legal History at Rutgers University. Among the numerous books he has authored or edited are *The Ballad of America, Trumpet of a Prophecy,* and *Teaching for a Change.*

Text set in Electra
Printed and bound by The Book Press, Brattleboro, Vt.
Series styled by Atha Tehon
This book designed by Elliot Epstein